Centered *by a* Miracle

A true story of
Friendship, Football, & Life

STEVE ROM & ROD PAYNE

SportsPublishingLLC.com

ISBN-10: 1-59670-145-5
ISBN-13: 978-1-59670-145-8
© 2006 by Steve Rom and Rod Payne

Publishers: Peter L. Bannon and Joseph J. Bannon Sr.
Senior managing editor: Susan M. Moyer
Acquisitions editor: Noah Amstadter
Developmental editor: Mark Newton
Art director: K. Jeffrey Higgerson
Dust jacket design: Heidi Norsen
Interior and insert layout: Heidi Norsen
Photo editor: Erin Linden-Levy

Sports Publishing L.L.C.
804 North Neil Street
Champaign, IL 61820
Phone: 1-877-424-2665
Fax: 217-363-2073
SportsPublishingLLC.com

Printed in the United States of America

CIP data available upon request.

*In memory of Pearl L. Cook, my grandmother and friend,
and to Mom, my teammate, now and forever.*

—S.R.

*"In everyone's life at some time, our inner fire goes out.
It is then burst into flame by an encounter with another
human being. We should all be thankful for those people
who rekindle the inner spirit."*

—ALBERT SCHWEITZER

Contents

CHAPTER ONE

Get Your Head on Straight

⊶ ⊱⬥⊰ ⊷

"What you do speaks so well, you don't have to say a word."
—Reggie McKenzie

I've been in the hospital a couple of days, I think; I don't really know. The morphine my doctors have been giving me for the pain has kicked in, zapping my short-term memory. The days blend together.

I can't think about anything, really, other than the disconcerting news I heard a couple of days ago—or however many days it's been.

The news arrived just after nightfall on December 26, 2001. It was delivered to me quickly, coldly, by an emergency room doctor I had just met.

"We examined your blood," he said, giving no sign of the wrecking ball headed my way, "and we think it might be leukemia."

Before hearing those words, I had fully expected this gray-haired man in a white coat to tell me to go home and sleep it off—"it" being the severe flu-like symptoms I'd been experiencing the previous three days. Instead, he was telling me to say good-bye to the life I had known—the one I had worked so hard for, the one back in Michigan.

The news still hasn't sunk in yet.

Leukemia?

After all I've been through as a kid?

When I was nine years old, I had a tumor removed from my spine. Seventy-five weeks of chemotherapy and full-body radiation followed before the doctors deemed me cured. It was a tough road, one that wasn't made any easier by being the only fourth-grader in my elementary school with no hair—kids can be cruel—but at least it came to an end.

I wonder how far this detour will take me off my life's path. I'm just 29 and on my way to becoming a successful, respected journalist. I don't know what's going to happen to me now.

All I know about leukemia—doctors are calling it ALL, or acute lymphoblastic leukemia—is what I learned from a story I wrote more than a year ago about a boy who had it. He had a different type of leukemia, but I'm guessing they're all in the same league: PDBD, or potentially deadly blood diseases.

Anders Nieters was a 14-year-old cyclist—15, actually, but his father, Jim, had lost track because Anders' many months of treatments had blended together, kind of like my days now.

For Jim, counting birthday candles quickly gave way to blood counts, pill counts, and counting the rare days his only son was out of the hospital. Full days—24 hours. Ambulance rides in the middle of the night didn't count.

While I think about Anders, and wonder how he's doing today, I watch a pair of nurses walk into my room. One comes over to my bed and, without saying a word, lifts my arm up by the wrist. She starts reading the information on my hospital ID band to the other nurse, who's standing across the room, staring at the label on a bag of blood she's cradling like a newborn baby. A moment later, the nurses repeat the process. This time the one carrying the blood reads aloud while the other stares at my wristband.

The more they ignore me, the more helpless I feel.

"Why do you keep reading my name?" I blurt out.

After a pause—as if they are shocked I even have a voice—the one holding my wrist responds. Without removing her eyes from my ID band, she says calmly, as if she's telling me the time, "Because you can die if you get the wrong blood."

Is that all? I can die if I get the wrong blood. What do you mean I can die if I get the wrong blood? Is she serious? How can she say something like that and be so nonchalant about it? I've never been more terrified in my life.

I'm having a blood transfusion—a standard procedure, I'm told. But the sight of someone else's beet-red blood seeping into my veins is more than I can bear. Soon, I feel a horrible metallic taste, which nearly makes me sick. It reminds me of when I was a kid and swallowed my own blood, either on purpose or accident, and first experienced that taste. Now it's different, because I can feel it throughout my entire body—and it's not my blood.

The nurse who told me I could die checks the drip coming through the IV tube. She flicks it with her finger, then lifts the extra tubing off the floor, coils it like a garden hose, and sets it on my bed. A moment later, she and the other nurse walk out of the room, neither offering a time frame for when this madness will end. I am on edge throughout the transfusion, which lasts nearly three hours.

When it finally does end—mercifully without incident—I give thanks, the most thanks I've ever given.

⊷ ⚎✦⚎ ⊶

The morphine keeps coming. So does the chemotherapy, which is so powerful it requires a nurse to wear blue rubber gloves, a white mask, and a yellow protective robe when administering it to me. Doctors dressed in the same attire (only their coats are blue) have been ordering this cocktail of drugs for me all day in hopes of ridding me of the diseased blood cells that have taken over my body and delivered me back here—"here" being the same university research hospital I left two decades ago, vowing never to return again.

I begin to stare, forlorn, through the window of my 10th-floor hospital room at the city I grew up in. It's a dark, cloudy day in Los Angeles, which reminds me even more of the unpleasant memories that reside here. I tried so hard to escape this city.

I thought I had escaped a few years earlier, when I became a student at the University of Michigan in Ann Arbor. It was the fall of 1998.

I've done well since the move, graduating for one (for a long time I thought that only happened to other people). I also found a new and exciting career as a sports journalist. That was another huge plus, considering the pair of short-lived careers I had back in LA—computer animator at Sony Pictures, and rock-and-roll bass player in Hollywood—only inspired me to return to school. (Dreams, I found, die hard on Hollywood Boulevard.)

Everything looked so promising after the move to my new life in Michigan. Now it seems to be slipping away as quickly as the chemotherapy and liquid food dripping through my IV tubes.

Before I have a chance to recover from what that nurse told me before my transfusion, I'm blindsided by the sight of another pair of nurses entering my room.

Another transfusion? Sadly, yes. One is holding a bag of blood. The nurses are different. The results, however, are the same: they begin reading; I begin fretting.

I can die if I get the wrong blood. I can die if I get the wrong blood. . . .

As the words ring out in my head, my vision suddenly goes askew. The nurse in charge of the blood bag no longer appears to be cradling a baby but rather a sidearm machine gun she's about to unload on me at close range.

And I can't stop thinking about those words.

"I can die if I get the wrong blood," I say to the nurses, and likely the entire wing of the oncology ward. "I had a transfusion yesterday. Nobody told me about another one. I don't need another one. Get my doctors in here. Now!"

Before long, the room is filled with people.

My family members look on in silence as doctors and nurses check my records, verify my patient ID number, my blood type, and that of the blood in the bag. My mom and grandmother are here, seated in chairs by the window. And my friend, Rod, is beside me, sitting atop a rickety, fold-up cot he's been sleeping on since arriving here shortly after that first transfusion.

Rod came out immediately after hearing the news. He flew in from Michigan, just like I did a couple weeks ago for what was supposed to be a short vacation home. I remember telling him the news, and I didn't have to be gentle with him like I did when I called my boss and girlfriend. Rod is no stranger to difficult news: he endured a dozen surgeries during a four-year NFL career.

Rod, who I've known just six months, already has a lot to do with that promising life I've been working so hard for. He's been like a mentor to me, sharing everything he knows about teamwork, discipline, dedication, pride—everything he's learned in football.

For now, however, Rod appears no different than the rest of the people in my hospital room: sitting there as calm as can be.

How can they be so calm?

Don't they know I can die if I get the wrong blood?

"I don't need a blood transfusion. No one told me I was going to get another one. Get out of here with that blood!"

I've created such a stir in my agitated state that nobody is at ease. As I continue my rant, I wonder when this sabotage will end and when somebody will tell me something or include me in what's going on.

Suddenly, Rod leaps to his feet, his 6-foot-4, 300-pound frame now revealed in earnest.

"Everyone, clear the room," he says in a deep, bellowing voice, pointing to the door. "I need to talk to him. Alone!" Everyone looks stunned, but no one moves. After taking a good look at Rod, however, and sensing his tension, they quickly scurry out. As the last person leaves, slowly closing the door from behind, I glance over at Rod. He's staring at me with daggers in his eyes, like a football coach about to berate a player for making a stupid move on the field.

"What's wrong with you?" he asks. "You have to trust what these doctors and nurses are doing. They're here to help you."

I don't answer. I just swallow and take a breath for the first time since glancing over.

"More importantly," Rod says, "you have to have faith in God. He is the only one in control of all this."

Rod pauses, then leans in closer.

"You have to get your head on straight!"

As his words hang in the air, Rod settles back into his cot. The lecture is over—for now.

Everyone returns to the room, proceeding slowly, cautiously, afraid to stir the easily roused giant. As they file back in, I pick a spot on the wall and don't take my eyes off it. And when the nurses begin reading the information on my ID band, I say nothing.

For the next three-plus hours, as the blood slowly disappears into my veins, I am oblivious to what's going on around me. With my eyes peering at the wall, I think about what Rod has told me and the reason why he's here.

Rod's not here for his health. He's here for mine.

CHAPTER TWO

Don't You Know Who This Is?

❦

"A minute's success pays the failure of years."
—ROBERT BROWNING

It was the summer of 2001, and I was a sports reporter at the *Ann Arbor News*. It was an exciting profession, but I found it exhausting trying to get ahead in the ultracompetitive field of journalism. Always having to track down the next story, forever trying to land "the scoop," wore me down physically and emotionally. I started to take every liberty I could to gain a much-needed, if only momentary, reprieve.

Because I missed my days as a student, I often frequented the same establishments I did when I lugged my dark gray backpack around campus. I went to the same bank, post office, dry cleaners, even hallmark Ann Arbor eateries: Mr. Spots for Philly cheesesteaks, Red Hot Lovers for Chicago dogs and waffle fries, and Pizza Bob's for buffalo wings and hot subs. Parking was always a premium on campus. Fortunately, I still lived close enough to walk there.

One day that summer, I left my apartment at 1313 South State Street, the main drag leading to campus from I-94 out of Detroit, as I did at least twice a week to do errands. My backpack was filled with letters and bills to be dropped off at the post office, clothes to be dry-cleaned, and withdrawal slips already filled out to get some quick cash from my checking account. I hadn't had an ATM card since I left LA. I didn't even have a car until I graduated in April 2000.

The best part of the 20-minute walk to campus—by far—was knowing I didn't have to stop at the library for the rest of the day (and sometimes night) to study some subject I had no interest in—namely economics, my major.

My original plan was to go back to Sony Pictures after graduating, this time on the business end of things. After a year and a half on the job at the old MGM Studios lot in Culver City, a couple miles from where I grew up, I was laid off along with 90 of my fellow computer animators. Companywide downsizing, I learned, is par for the course in the world of film and television production. Yet I didn't remember many executives being shown the door during that mass exodus from Sony in autumn 1997.

Because I missed the deadline to apply for Michigan's undergraduate business school, I was placed into the College of Literature, Science, and the Arts (LS&A). I decided to study economics—a discipline offered in the LS&A program—because I enjoyed the entry-level micro and macro classes I took at my community college after leaving Sony. I figured it would get me on track to receiving a business education. It didn't; it derailed me. I ended up hating economics.

Thankfully, my days of struggling over game theory and supply-and-demand curves were over.

For some reason, the vintage red brick building directly across the street from me caught my eye. It was the Marie Hartwig Building, a two-story, half-block-long structure named after the University of Michigan's first female athletic director. It rests near the corner of the first major intersection I came across on my trip to do errands. I'd passed by the building dozens of times but never paid much attention to it until then.

The athletic ticket office is located there, as well as the offices of the athletic department's coaches and administrators. I stopped and looked at the building. As I did, I was reminded of something one of the top administrators housed there said to me at a Michigan women's basketball game the previous season.

I was at Crisler Arena, which is named after another former AD, Fritz Crisler, and was reporting on the game for the *Ann Arbor News*. At halftime, I bumped into Jamie Morris, a former Michigan football player turned director of sports marketing. He was standing with friends by the tunnel leading to the locker rooms. I joked with him about how some early arriving students chanted his name when he walked across the court before the game: *"Ja-mie! Ja-mie! Ja-mie!"*

"You're a star," I said, smiling.

Jamie offered no rebuttal. Instead, he gave me a firm handshake.

"How've you been?" he asked.

"Good. And you?"

"Great, man," Jamie said, patting me on the back. People were watching. I felt important.

When Jamie finally released my hand, I said so long and headed for the steps leading to the concourse, where I fetched the free hot dog, popcorn, and soda we reporters got for covering the game.

"Stop by my office anytime, Steve," Jamie said as I rushed away. "Just to talk."

"Will do," I replied, then soared up the arena's stairs.

Later, as I sat with my fellow reporters at press row, digesting my dogs—I always finagled an extra one—I thought about how amazing it was to have received Jamie's invitation, even though I never intended to use it.

Jamie and I got along, sure. We even patted each other on the back at basketball games. But I was a reporter. Times had long gone when athletes and reporters were friends who hung out together after games, downed beers at the corner bar, and exchanged juicy secrets. Secrets like those are printed in newspapers the next morning under banner headlines. These days, athletes make so much money people want to know about their indiscretions. And people buy papers;

athletes don't. (You hear it all time: "I never read what you guys write.")

Jamie, though long retired, was an athlete. He played in the NFL with the Washington Redskins. And until a year earlier, he was Michigan's all-time leading rusher, his title surrendered to Anthony "A-Train" Thomas late in the 2000 season. I interviewed Thomas after his final game at Michigan Stadium, as more than 100,000 fans cheered him off the field. You can bet A-Train and I didn't get together later that night to talk about what a thrill that moment was for him—and me.

In fact, a veteran coworker had recently warned me about the pitfalls of such journalistic blasphemy.

"Don't get too close to the athletes you cover," my coworker said, sounding like an elder warrior sharing his wisdom with a noble young soldier. "You have to keep your distance from them."

I suppose he was saying that distance allows us to write about them without letting emotions get in the way.

Athletes compete; we write about them. Those were the simple mechanics of the system. Everybody was happy.

I was happy too—at least I thought I was—until the sunny day I found myself standing across the street from the Marie Hartwig Building, where Jamie sat in his office. It made me think about the great divide between athletes and reporters and the reasons why it exists. As I resumed my march to campus, something besides the red brick building caught my eye.

I watched the busy lunchtime traffic clear, and it was like something was forcing me to cross the street. I felt pulled to the other side, even though I still viewed Jamie's offer as professional courtesy more than any real invitation to visit him socially. Whether that was true or not, at that moment, I didn't really care.

It was a nice day; I didn't have to go to the library; and I wanted to talk.

After walking past the secretary's desk inside the plush building, I headed down the hall to Jamie's office. I'd been in the building before to interview some of the coaches of the teams I covered for the paper, mostly women's sports and the rest of Michigan's "nonrevs." Those are the sports such as swimming, soccer, track and field, and all of the so-called Olympic sports that make the university little or no revenue. As I closed in on Jamie's office, I noticed the door was cracked open.

I hesitated, began to turn around, and had to remind myself what Jamie had told me: stop by *anytime* to talk. Well, this was anytime.

As I approached the door, I took a deep breath and poked my head inside. Just then, I noticed Jamie was sitting with someone—someone who looked like a football player himself.

He was wearing a dark-blue T-shirt with MICHIGAN in yellow letters parading across the chest, the kind sold in all of the campus bookstores.

I pardoned the interruption and tried to excuse myself, but Jamie invited me to come in.

"This is Rod Payne," he said, motioning at his visitor.

"Nice to meet you, Rob," I said as I shook hands with the man.

"Rob?" Jamie said, springing to his feet and practically lunging over his desk in the process. "Don't you know who this is?"

I glanced again at the fellow. He was seated by the window, looking out over the intramural track, where the old football stadium, Ferry Field, used to be. People were sitting on the infield grass, having lunch as joggers circled by. Besides the double-XL T-shirt, I saw he was wearing baggy shorts, flip-flops, and a black NFL cap turned backward. He looked like a student.

"Oh, do you play football here?" I said.

"Maaaan, this is Rod Payne!" Jamie said, falling back into his chair. "He *used* to play here. He was MVP in '96! He just won the Super Bowl with the Ravens!"

"The *Baltimore* Ravens?" I wondered.

I remembered watching the game from the *News'* sports department a few months prior. It was one of the most entertaining Super Bowls I'd ever seen—Baltimore completely demolished the

New York Giants, 34–7. The game was so lopsided, in fact, the most dramatic part of it (besides the coin toss) was Britney Spears performing with Aerosmith at halftime in a skin-tight NFL jersey.

As I scrambled to come up with an excuse for my ignorance—I was a sportswriter and a Michigan graduate, so I should have known who Rod was—Jamie let me off the hook.

"What does he know?" Jamie asked his VIP guest. "He's from LA."

We all laughed for what seemed like a minute. I was grateful the tension had been expunged from the room instead of me.

After apologizing for my flub, I prepared to make my exit when Jamie invited me to sit down. I took the chair next to Rod. Jamie told me Rod was from Miami and that he was now retired—though it looked to me like he could've played another 10 years.

"Where you from in LA?" Rod asked, catching me off guard. I thought he'd just nod in my direction and get back to his conversation with Jamie.

"I was in LA for the Rose Bowl," Rod said before I could answer. "During my freshman year in '92."

"Really?" I said.

"I remember we ate at this prime rib place in Beverly Hills," Rod added, smiling at the thought. "They shut it down for our whole team. We had these huge slices that chefs cut for us off silver carts."

"Lawry's," I said, knowing it hosts the Rose Bowl teams each year. "I've been there before—lots of times."

"Yeah, that's it."

Rod seemed different from the other athletes I met through my job. He was interested in me, like I was an actual person—not a reporter, not the enemy.

"So you work at the *Ann Arbor News*?" Rod asked. "How long have you been there?"

"I started right after the beginning of my senior year. I graduated in 2000, so a couple years."

"You like being a reporter?"

"Yeah. I get to meet a lot of cool people." Maybe I wasn't being completely honest, but I suddenly felt a little more positive about my job.

"Why'd you come all the way out here for school?" Rod asked.

"Mostly because UCLA turned me down. I wanted to go there because it was right up the road from where I lived. I even had a B average at my community college, so they should have accepted me."

"You don't want to go to UCLA," Rod said.

"I know. After I saw this place, I felt like writing UCLA a thank-you letter for turning me down."

I asked Rod why he decided to come to Michigan, thinking he probably could have gone to school anywhere.

"I wanted to try something new," he said. "It was funny, everyone called me crazy for coming to the cold. But I actually liked it. It was different."

"Sounds familiar," I said. "LA will always be there for me. It never changes."

"Yeah, so will sunny Miami."

I was starting to forget that Rod was actually a Super Bowl champion. Although I was in awe of the sacrifices he must have made to reach such lofty heights in athletics, the pure dedication it took, I was more amazed by his gregarious personality. I found it rare for someone of his status—and stature. Rod was nearly twice my size.

"So, what are you going to do now that you're retired?" I asked him.

"I was thinking about becoming a screenwriter," he said.

"Really?"

Actually, I was thinking, "Great. Another football player trying to get into film."

"I used to work at Sony Pictures in LA, doing special effects for film and TV." I told him. "Do you have some stories you're working on now?"

"Yeah. A whole bunch."

"Can I hear one? I won't steal it, I'm just curious. I saw a lot of screenplays at Sony. I was there almost two years."

Jamie's phone rang. As he took the call and settled into the conversation, Rod started to break down a film he wrote about a group of friends. It opened with them hanging out in a coffee shop.

"Oh boy, *Friends*, the movie," I was thinking. But as Rod painted the picture, described the characters in the scene, then led them out of the shop and into a van, he grabbed my attention.

"Two of the guys in the back pull out ski masks," Rod said, leaning in closer. "'You ready to do this?' one asked the other. 'No, wait till we get there,' the driver said, as he eased the van into traffic. 'Just be patient. We'll have plenty of time to get ready.'"

Although the story might have rung too closely to *Point Break*, I still was impressed. I felt like I was in that van with the friends on the way to the heist, or wherever Rod was about to lead me.

The more of the story Rod told, the more it felt like I was in a theater looking up at the big screen, not in Jamie's office. I started to realize that Rod not only played football but had other skills as well. He was a great storyteller—and writer, apparently.

"Maybe I can put you in touch with some people I know out at Sony," I told him.

"Sounds good."

We exchanged e-mail addresses and phone numbers. As Rod took my business card and put it in his wallet, he shot me a curious look.

"You're not 22 are you?" Rod asked.

"Oh, you did the math?" I said, cracking a smile. "I took a few years off after high school. I spent five years playing in rock bands before I went to Sony. I'm actually 28."

"I knew it," Rod said, letting out a hearty chuckle.

Jamie was still on the phone, so Rod and I continued our conversation.

"Do you have any family out here?" he asked me.

"No. My parents divorced when I was really young. My mom's in LA, and I don't have any brothers or sisters. My dad's in Arizona. He and his second wife just retired there from Minnesota, where I was born."

"Yeah, I'm an only child too," Rod said. "I was raised by my mother."

"So your parents divorced when you were young?" I asked.

"I was about two."

"Is your mom still in Miami?"

"Yeah. She works at the post office."

"My mom works in an orthopedic surgery office. She actually works for the doctor for the LA Clippers. The players come into her office all the time. They used to take me into the locker room when I was a kid. Norm Nixon, Bill Walton, they used to know me back then. They still ask about me."

"Really? Bill Walton?"

Rod leaned back in his chair, smiling. Jamie finally ended his call.

"So what have you two been talking about?" Jamie asked.

"Nothing," Rod said.

As I prepared to excuse myself—I didn't want to wear out my welcome—Rod and I shook hands again. This time I made sure to call him Rod, and I told him I'd keep in touch.

"Great," he said. "It was good meeting you."

When I got home after finishing my errands, I rushed to my laptop and typed Rod's e-mail and phone number into my Excel spreadsheet—the important contacts file. I thought I might be able to write a story about his return to Ann Arbor and made a mental note to talk to my bosses about it when I got into work later.

In the meantime, I continued to marvel at the conversation I'd had with Rod. For the first time in a while, I actually felt like a human being again, not a human tape recorder.

CHAPTER THREE

Run the Ball!

* ⇥◆⇤ *

"Leadership is action, not position."
—Donald H. McGannon

After folding the last of the laundry I'd been putting off for weeks, I threw on a shirt and headed to the recycling bins behind my apartment to get rid of some old newspapers.

As I walked along the dirt- and pebble-covered driveway, I noticed a large black man walking toward me. He was coming from the parking lot my roommate, Arun, and I shared with the house next door. Consumed in thought, I barely lifted my head while nodding hello to the stranger as he passed.

"Where'd you get that shirt?"

The booming voice coming from behind startled me. I stopped and looked down to see what I had just put on. When I recognized the Super Bowl XXXV logo and the Ravens and Giants helmets, I started to place the voice.

"Don't I know you?" I said, turning toward the fellow. "Yeah, we met in Jamie Morris' office about a month ago."

Chances are Rod and I would have walked in and out of each other's lives again had it not been for the T-shirt my mom, Paula, had sent me from Los Angeles.

Mom always sent me T-shirts, mostly from sports championships—NBA Finals, World Series. It's been a tradition of hers since I left for college: she goes to the mall and buys them the day they come out. Knowing I'm wearing them, I think, makes her feel closer to me.

Upon a closer look, I noticed Rod's boyish features, those that belied his age and level of success and caused me to think he was still a student when we met.

As I walked up to Rod, I remembered I had promised to e-mail him. I felt embarrassed for not having followed through.

"I was planning on calling you," I said as I shook his hand. "Sorry, man."

"I was gonna call you too," Rod said. "Oh man, things have been crazy." I could only imagine the fanfare over Rod's return to town.

"No, I should have called you," I said. "I've been meaning to write that story on you."

"Oh yeah?"

Before Rod offered another word, he showed me his new ring.

"It just came in the mail," he said.

While my eyes feasted on the huge hunk of diamonds and gold wrapped around his finger, Rod twisted the ring off and dropped it into my hand. It was the size of a golf ball, bigger even, the first Super Bowl ring I'd ever seen up close, let alone held. It was heavy like a paperweight. It took my breath away.

"You live over there?" Rod asked, pointing to the building behind me.

"Yeah," I said, not taking my eyes off the jewelry. "With my roommate."

I couldn't believe the detail of the ring. It had the score of the game (34–7) on the side, just below the Super Bowl XXXV logo. The other side read PAYNE 59—his number—in banner type. The top was a football field made of diamonds with the Ravens' logo in the middle consisting of purple stones (with a red one for the eye). I fired the image of that sparkling Ravens logo into my brain, never wanting to forget what a thrill it was to hold the ring.

I carefully handed it back and thanked Rod for showing it to me.

"So what brings you here?" I asked.

"I'm visiting one of my boys next door."

"Right there?" I asked, pointing to the one-story house behind Rod.

"Yeah," he said, then told me his friend who lived there was a former Michigan football player.

"Oh really?" I had often seen him and his friends hanging out on the porch, but I'd never talked to them.

Rod and I caught up for another minute, after which I apologized again for not having contacted him. I was already making a mental note to e-mail him later in the week when he interrupted my thoughts again.

"I'm gonna go see my boy, then I'll drop by after I'm done."

"Drop by where? Our place?" I wondered. I had expected Rod just to say, "Take care of yourself. See you around."

"Cool," I said calmly, even though my heart was in my throat.

I pointed to the two doors on the second floor of 1313, which always made me think of 1313 Mockingbird Lane from *The Munsters*. "We're on the left side, apartment 2A."

After throwing out the newspapers, I rushed inside to tell Arun who was coming over.

⊷ ⊶⊰⊱⊷ ⊶

Arun Gopal, a premed student and a former coworker at the *Michigan Daily*, our college newspaper, was busy fixing a bowl of cereal when I told him the news. Arun was still a reporter at the *Daily*.

That fall, he would begin covering Michigan football, the best beat at the paper.

"Guess who's coming over?"

"Who?" Arun asked, pushing his trademark glasses higher up the bridge of his nose.

"Rod Payne," I announced.

Arun's look of amazement said it all.

Arun was a Michigan native, and like any Michigander can tell you—as long as he didn't grow up in an ice-fishing shed somewhere in the Upper Peninsula—Michigan football is as much a part of the fabric of the state as Ford and Motown. So Arun, a lifelong Michigan football fan, knew all about Rod.

"Payne is hilarious!" Arun said. "He's like the Charles Barkley of college football."

"No kidding?"

"He really had a knack of hamming it up with reporters. It was legendary."

"That's what some of my coworkers at the *News* said."

I hadn't told Arun about my first meeting with Rod, like I did a few reporters at work. Some of them had been around when Rod made his mark at Michigan in the mid-1990s. Rod's rants were so plentiful, they said, he was often the first player the media rushed to in the locker room after games. But one performance, they all agreed, stands out—and it happened at a Michigan State press conference.

I was about to ask Arun if he'd heard the story when there was a knock at the door.

"That might be Rod," I said. "Maybe his friend's not home."

I was right.

After I greeted Rod at the door, I watched him navigate his way to the kitchen, where he fished out a can of beer from deep in the lower shelf of the refrigerator. It was a leftover from a rare get-together Arun and I had had the previous weekend with friends, mostly *Daily* sportswriters.

As Rod cracked open the beer, I took a seat on the couch next to Arun. He and I watched our guest continue to make himself at home, which helped us forget, if only for a moment, the unrelenting heat and humidity of a typical Ann Arbor summer afternoon.

"Damn, it's hot in here," Rod said, taking a monster-size swig of his beer. He stood in the middle of the living room, studying the furniture layout.

"You guys have the air conditioner on?"

"Yep," we both said.

It was gasping, full bore, per usual. Rod shook his head and took another swig. He thought for a moment then suggested we go sit outside.

"Might as well," he said, already heading for the door. "It's just as hot in here."

Arun and I peeled ourselves off the couch. We ran to the kitchen and battled for the last beer in the fridge, which we quickly agreed to split.

We joined Rod on the stairwell of the mostly student-filled apartment we moved into the previous fall, the first fall after my graduation. As we took a seat on the steps, I realized this was the first time Arun and I had sat outside and shared a beer, a moment, since we moved in. This was partly because of our competing schedules, but mostly because we hadn't made the time to get to know each other.

Rod was already comfortable on the steps when we sat down. I wasted no time in renewing the conversation we had begun in Jamie's office.

"What's this I hear about the Michigan State press conference?" I said, cracking open the last beer.

"You heard about that?" Rod said.

"Yeah, some of my coworkers remember it. They didn't tell me too much about it, though. They just said it was hysterical."

"It was my senior year," Rod said, taking another drink of his beer. Behind him, cars whizzed by on South State Street. "I was captain, and the captains are always interviewed during the press conferences leading up to the games."

I could picture Rod at the dais in the media room at Crisler Arena, a giant *M* logo behind him, all of those reporters and cameramen looking on. I'd been in that room many times for postgame interviews with the women's basketball coaches and players.

"A reporter asked me what it meant for the seniors to be playing our in-state rival for the last time. So I pulled out my wallet and started searching through it. I didn't say anything. Everyone was looking at me like, 'What the hell is he doing?'"

Arun, I noticed, was hanging on every word. So was I.

"So I looked through the wallet, taking my time, then pulled out a credit card," Rod continued. "I held it up and said, 'Guys, see this? This is all you need to know about this game on Saturday. We hate Michigan State so much we won't use any cash this week, because we don't want to even touch anything green.'"

"What happened when you said that?" Arun asked.

"Everybody busted out laughing," Rod said.

I imagine they did. Those midweek press conferences are normally a borefest. While they're supposed to drum up attention for the upcoming game, players and coaches are usually so guarded they never say anything good in fear of giving the opponent an edge, or even worse, providing them with "bulletin-board material." I heard Michigan head coach Lloyd Carr even tells his players not to say anything that can be construed as antagonizing or he'll bench them.

"That's an amazing story," I said. I took another sip of the beer and passed it to Arun.

"That's nothing," Rod said. "You want to know what I did when we played Ohio State?"

Did we? The Ohio State game is the highlight of every season—10 times more important than the Michigan State game.

"I hear that game's so big, people schedule weddings and funerals around it," I said, recalling an article I had read the previous fall in *USA Today*.

"Oh yeah," Rod said. "This is a game that people ask us about all week long. Wherever we go: 'You gonna win the game? What's up with the game, man?' There's a lot of pressure. In fact, none of the players even go to class that week so we can just focus on the Buckeyes. I mean not one! We just wake up, eat, and go to the Building."

The Building, I knew, was Schembechler Hall, the team's state-of-the-art training facility. Its three perfectly manicured practice fields, which are guarded by a 12-foot brick wall, were directly behind Rod in the distance. The rest of the facility, including the indoor field, was about a half block north of us. I thought that was where Rod was going when I ran into him in the parking lot.

"So we were playing Ohio State, and we *had* to win that game," Rod said. "And we played horribly. I had to tell the coaches to change their game plan—right there on the sideline."

"What was the problem?" I asked. "Why were you playing so badly?"

Rod was quick with his answer.

"We were passing the ball too much. We had three first-half interceptions. I came off the field after the third one, went right up to the coaches and screamed, 'What are you doing? We're going to lose this game! Let's run the ball—punch 'em in the mouth!'"

"Three yards and a cloud of dust," I said, recalling the mantra of Michigan's teams of yesteryear.

"Absolutely," Rod said. He seemed happy I knew that.

"See, if you run the ball, it shows confidence. It allows you to impose your will at the line of scrimmage. Those are the trenches, where games are won and lost. The defense gets tired if you keep pounding them by running the ball. You can see them, hands on their hips, sucking wind as they walk up to the line."

"So what happened with the game?" I asked.

"We ended up winning, and we ran for 400 yards. Check the statistics. That's crazy for a team to have three first-half interceptions and still run for 400 yards. I told the coaches all week we should do that, but they didn't listen."

Rod didn't seem to be gloating. Rather, it sounded like he was still reacting in shock that it actually came to him having to challenge his coaches' authority in front of a national TV audience.

"It's cool the coaches listened to you," I told Rod. "It's cool that you stepped up too."

"Actually, that was the consensus of a lot of the guys on the team. Plus, it was my job to speak up."

Rod crushed his empty beer can and set it next to him on the step.

"If I wasn't the player I was, if I gave a half-hearted effort, I wouldn't have ever been MVP or team captain, and my coaches wouldn't have listened to me."

I can only imagine the confidence Rod had working for him during that Ohio State game. It had to help knowing he was playing for a program with well over a century of success. I remember the *Ann Arbor News* printed a series of stories leading up to Michigan's NCAA-record 800th victory the previous season. We chronicled the program's rich history, including how the Wolverines played in the very first Rose Bowl game on January 1, 1902. They beat Stanford 49–0 in front of horse-drawn carriages.

"At Michigan, there's a code we live by," Rod said. "It's that the expectation is for the position. That means the individual is taken out of the equation. It makes it so that the person who wears the helmet, who plays the position, is held to the same standard as everyone else who came before him.

"For a very short time, a continuation of tradition is in your hands. And you don't want to be the one who doesn't perpetuate that tradition."

Rod paused to let those words settle.

"You guys live in a great location," he said, breaking the silence. The sun was beginning to set behind Rod, the cars appearing less frequently.

"It's great on game day," I said, "everybody walking to the stadium, people having barbecues. It's like one big block party."

"I'm sure it is," Rod said. "Speaking of that, do you have any more beers?"

"No," I told him. "But we can go to the store."

"That's OK," Rod replied. "So how do you guys like being reporters? You say you're covering football in the fall?" Rod looked at Arun.

"Um, yeah," Arun said, his voice slightly cracking. I took the beer out of Arun's hand, but he didn't look at me. He was transfixed by Rod.

"That's cool," Rod said. "I've been talking with producers at WTKA about becoming a cohost on their afternoon drive time show."

"So you're thinking about crossing over to the dark side?" I asked. We all laughed.

WTKA was the big sports talk-radio station in town. I rarely listened to it, but I was sure Rod would add a lot to the programming.

I was about to ask Rod about the status of his hire when he shared some of the encounters he had with the local sportswriters while playing at Michigan.

"A few of them were cool," Rod said about those from the two major Detroit papers (the *Detroit News* and *Detroit Free Press*) and the *Ann Arbor News*. "There are some good writers out here, but a lot of those guys are knuckleheads, too. They'll write anything just to advance their own careers. I had some teammates that wanted to beat some of those dudes up for what they wrote, stories that had information they shared in confidence. That's why a lot of these writers were never athletes—they don't understand the importance of camaraderie. In football, that's more important than anything, even winning and losing."

Arun and I sat silently as Rod indicted our fellow reporters. Despite how fired up Rod became, we felt no trepidation. It was clear he was not accusing us for the negligence of our peers but simply warning us of the prevalent pitfalls of our trade.

Even with the rant, it seemed Rod looked at us differently than he did the writers who give our profession a bad name. Maybe that was because he had retired or because we were sharing a beer with him, not jamming a tape recorder in his face by his locker after a game.

After an hour sitting on the steps, Rod announced he had to go.

"I have a party to get ready for over at Scorekeepers," he said, referring to one of the downtown sports bars.

I knew about the party. It was an invite-only for Michigan football players and friends, part of the annual Charles Woodson–Jim Harbaugh charity golf tournament in town. Both were former Michigan standouts and NFL veterans. I interviewed Woodson, the 1997 Heisman Trophy–winner, at the previous year's golf tournament after he was arrested for drunk driving the night before its start. The story was a scoop by the *Ann Arbor News*. It went national and landed me a promotion at work.

"You guys want to come to the party?" Rod asked after standing up and stretching his back for a good 10 seconds.

It had already been the most enjoyable hour Arun and I had spent together that summer, and then Rod invited us to meet up with him later at the VIP party?

"Just tell the security guy at the door you're with me," he instructed, then thanked us for the beer and hustled down the stairs into the quickly fading afternoon.

"See y'all later," Rod said, turning the corner into the driveway.

When Arun and I went inside, I wondered whether I would run into Woodson at the party. After talking with Rod and seeing how cool he was, I wanted to thank Woodson for talking to me after his arrest.

I was the only reporter Woodson did talk to, which is why the story went national. If it hadn't been for that, I wouldn't have been covering women's basketball the previous season. It was part of my promotion, along with a weekly "College Notes" column (tidbits about the nonrev sports) and my picture in the paper. And if I hadn't been spending so much time at Crisler Arena the previous winter, I'd never have met Jamie—and in turn, Rod.

I didn't spend much time thinking about my good fortune, however. I had things to do. I had to put away my laundry, make something to eat, and get ready for the party.

"Are you going?" I asked Arun after sharing my plans.

"Heck yeah!" he said, giving me a look that said I was crazy for even asking.

CHAPTER FOUR

Do You Play Football?

· ·◄◆►· ·

"Civilization degrades the many to exalt the few."
—AMOS BRONSON ALCOTT

od's Army-style cot has just arrived. A hospital orderly wheels it into my room, like we're at a hotel on vacation. My grandmother, Nana I call her, tips the man. I admonish her for doing it. That's his job.

As Rod sets up the contraption and attempts to get comfortable in it, a feat I don't think even he can achieve (his feet are dangling clear off the end), Mom and Nana tell me they're leaving for the day. I say goodbye and begin scanning the channels of the television hanging from the ceiling in the corner of my room.

Nothing grabs me as I click away on the remote control, which is connected to the wall by a thick, rubber cord. The cord is short, so it keeps yanking the remote out of my hand.

I look over at Rod—he's still trying to get settled in his cot. How admirable. I've already given up trying to get comfortable in my bed, which is so soft and porous it sucks me in like quicksand.

Suddenly, I hit the jackpot: ESPN.

Wouldn't you know it—a boring afternoon filler program—not the repeat of last night's *SportsCenter* I wanted to watch. I quickly ditch it in search of (could I be so lucky?) a movie channel.

"Let me see the remote," Rod says as he places his cell phone, wallet, and Super Bowl ring next to the Kleenex box on my nightstand.

"I got it," I say as Rod shifts his weight around the cot, still trying to get comfortable. "I'll find us something to watch."

Seeing Rod struggle, I begin to appreciate my adjustable bed with guardrails and plastic sheets a lot more, even though my backless hospital gown makes my butt stick to the sheets.

Having Rod here also makes me appreciate something else.

It feels like we're back in my apartment in Ann Arbor, where we've had so many good times over the last six months.

⊶ ⊰⊱ ⊷

Rod came over to 1313 a lot after his first visit that afternoon of the VIP party. (Arun and I did go to the party, by the way, and I did run into Woodson. I thanked him for talking to me after his arrest. "No problem," he said, a cigar in one hand, a girl in the other [two girls, actually], and then asked me how my career was going. Not as good as his social life, I was thinking.)

With Arun on campus most of the time—all those premed summer school classes—Rod and I spent a lot of time getting to know each other.

Our friendship began as one of sharing: Rod shared amazing stories of his life in football, and I shared a welcoming ear and a genuine appreciation of his athletic achievements. The football stories, however, quickly became springboards to more meaningful discussions. We talked about family, career, culture—everything—even girls, self-confidence, and fashion.

For a sportswriter, listening to Rod's stories about football at Michigan, in the pros, and in the Super Bowl was like a dream. They're stories you don't read about in newspapers, or see on nightly highlight reels—fun stories, like the one about the room full of gourmet food awaiting players and coaches at the Ravens' team hotel before the Super Bowl in Tampa.

"All the lobster and pineapple you could eat," Rod said, looking like he could enjoy some of that fare right then. "An entire room of it. I'm not kidding. We all stayed in that room for an hour before we went to our own rooms."

"That must have been nice," I said, lobster having always been one of my favorite foods.

"It got better when we got to our rooms," Rod said.

"What do you mean?"

"We had all the Super Bowl stuff you can think of: sweatshirts, hats, a computer bag, even a handheld video camera. And it wasn't just the players who got the stuff. Everyone who went to the Super Bowl did: family members, team personnel. Even the secretaries went to the Super Bowl. Some teams don't even send their practice-squad players to the game."

Although stories like these entertained me, Rod's tales about life—his climb to success, mostly, and how he did it—really fascinated me. Growing up, I never had a father around on a daily basis to share such vital stories with me and, in time, show me exactly how to make my own.

I told this to Rod one day in my apartment while we were sharing our pasts. We did that a lot.

"My dad told me about his insurance company in Minnesota, the one he took over from his dad, every once in a while. And that he used to design model cars, winning all kinds of awards as a kid. But other than that, not much—oh, and he was in the Navy. I know that because I've seen pictures. But he didn't tell me anything about that either, like what he learned from it, why he went into the Navy in the first place, or anything."

"How old were you when your parents divorced?" Rod asked.

"I was about nine months. My mom and I moved to Los Angeles a year later. I told you I was born in Minnesota, right? She married a man who lived out there: Pops, I call him. That marriage lasted only a few years, leaving me right back where I started."

"I was right there with you," Rod said. He attempted to find a comfortable position on the couch. It was still very hot in the apartment. The balcony door behind him was wide open. "My mom remarried—I was about 10—but that didn't last long. So I never really had a father around. All of my coaches were my fathers."

Though I've never been an athlete, I understood what Rod meant.

I've heard coaches all my life—first on TV, then in person when I became a reporter—refer to their players as their "kids" or "my sons" and say they'd do anything for them.

"I did have some people in my life, like my stepfather, Myron— that's Pops. He always told me to do something I like as a career. 'Do something in sports,' he'd say, but I never listened. I always thought it was too late, because I was in high school when he said it."

"It's never too late," Rod says. "I didn't start playing football until my junior year in high school. And I had asthma growing up, so I had to deal with that."

That was surprising to me; Rod looked so healthy. I decided I shouldn't ask him anything about it, though. I didn't want to pry. I also didn't tell him about my medical history. My cancer had been buried so far in my past, it was like it hadn't happened.

"So you never even saw your real father?" Rod asked.

"I used to visit him in the summers. But I was just a kid then, so we never had any real heart-to-hearts. All we did was eat at fast-food restaurants—McDonald's, Dairy Queen—and go to the state fair, Minnesota Twins games, and some Vikings game. So it really was my stepfather I spent more time with, and that wasn't all that often."

"Did you play any sports as a kid?" Rod asked.

"I could have been a pretty good baseball player," I said. "I was good at rec softball when I got older. And I won a gold glove in the Sony softball league for my stellar play in centerfield, if I do say so. But I never had what it took to try out for a team when I was young, when it mattered most."

"What about your parents? Didn't they tell you to play?"

"Not really. But I never really told them I wanted to play sports. It was just one of the many things I wanted to do as a kid that never came to fruition—like playing guitar. I've always loved music. I went to my first heavy metal concert when I was 12—Ratt, on New Year's Eve 1985 at the Long Beach Arena. I thought it was so awesome, seeing those guys do their thing in front of an arena full of people. But I never thought I could do it."

"That's crazy," Rod said.

"Yeah, I know. Now."

"So when did you start playing rock and roll?"

"After high school. First I tried community college, but that didn't work out. It felt like the 13th grade: a bunch of slackers ditching school to go to the beach. Plus, I was starting to think I had worn out my welcome in LA. I always felt I should have grown up in the Midwest, in that two-story suburban house Dad bought for us before the divorce. So I decided to move back to Minnesota and live with Dad and his wife in that house. I drove my car there—this cherry-red Camaro; it was my first car—and enrolled at the University of Minnesota—the 'U,' they call it there, not 'U-M,'" I explained.

"No kidding? You were a Golden Gopher? How long were you at Minnesota?"

"Just one quarter—winter 1991. I hated it at Minnesota too. I realized that the life I should have had there was long gone. Plus, my dad and I weren't getting along; he was treating me like a child. I think it was because he had never spent any time with me as an adult. He wanted to know where I was going, when I was coming home. He even gave me a curfew. I was 19 and had practically raised myself."

"I can understand that," Rod said.

"There was just no seeing eye-to-eye with him, so I got fed up and moved back to LA. I bought a guitar, grew my hair long, and decided to become a rock star—take over the world. I felt like there was something more for me in life, something special."

"That's quite a story," Rod said, resting comfortably on the couch.

━━◈━━

Shortly after Rod and I began hanging out, I realized the only difference between us was that Rod had eventually learned all of his lessons of manhood—and gained the qualities of pride, discipline, and hard work ethic—from his coaches. I, on the other hand, never had learned them.

Perhaps recognizing that, Rod decided to take on a big brother role with me—even though I was almost two years his senior. He tried to teach me things. Sometimes it was just patience or not jumping to conclusions, which he said his coaches often stressed to him.

I learned this lesson one night as Rod and I watched ESPN in my apartment.

"You hear that noise upstairs?" I said to Rod, who was sitting next to me on the couch, staring intently at the TV. "It's the same thing I heard last night!"

"Don't get so excited," Rod said.

"What do you mean? Listen to that. It's almost 1 a.m. Listen. Doesn't it sound like the neighbors are moving furniture around? How can they do that every night?"

"How do you know they're moving furniture?" Rod asked, still locked on the TV. "Don't just assume that's what's going on."

"What else could it be?"

I was so frustrated, I stood up and started pacing the living room.

"I should go up there and see what's going on."

"So do it; don't talk about it. Now get out of the way. You're in front of the TV."

Rod either had some extremely thick skin or just bad ears. I was trying to figure out which. Actually, I was more interested in figuring out what was happening with the happy-feet movers upstairs, those two or three Michigan students who, for whatever reason, I never ran into. I decided they must have had afternoon classes and stayed up all night.

A couple of days later, I ran into them. I was coming home from work as they jetted down the stairs and headed in the direction of campus on foot. Shortly after I went inside, the furniture started moving again.

"How can this be? I just saw them leave," I wondered aloud in frustration.

I stood up and followed the sound, which led me to the wall at the back of the living room. After pressing my ear against the wall, I realized it hadn't been the furniture moving around every night, but rather the pipes in the walls of the building making odd noises.

I told Rod about it the next day. He barely reacted.

"Oh, yeah," he said. "I told you not to get all excited."

I remember thinking it was almost as if Rod knew all along it was the pipes but wanted me to figure it out for myself.

After experiencing a few more of these epiphanies, I found it easier to listen to Rod. I always listened to him, even though he sometimes came at me loudly, angrily, or in front of people.

"Stop slouching," he would say when he noticed me sinking into the couch at one of his friend's apartments. And although this often made me angry, I always did what he said. I did it even though other people Rod tried to lecture—usually those he'd known a lot longer than me—told him to take his advice and stick it where he put his toilet paper.

Why did I put up with it?

I thought of the countelss times I returned home after school to an empty apartment as a kid. An empty apartment doesn't tell you to sit up on the couch, or ask you how your day was or whether you're having problems at school you need to talk about. I knew Rod wasn't trying to put me down. He was trying to teach me something, like his coaches always did for him.

"I came to high school one day wearing a new Dallas Cowboys hat. It was blue, and my coach started yelling at me because I wasn't wearing green and gold," Rod said.

"Green and gold?"

"Our class colors. 'What are our colors?' Coach asked. 'What are Killian's colors?' I said, 'Green and gold.' 'Then why aren't you wearing green and gold?' he shouted at me."

"He sounds like a drill sergeant."

"Yeah he was tough. But you know what? That weekend he took me to the mall and bought me an Oakland A's hat. He wanted to make sure I got the message. He said, 'Here, wear this. Don't ever let me see you wearing a hat that's not green and gold.'

"I was mad at first. But I learned a lot from that experience and a lot of others about pride and loyalty. I also had to humble myself, because I liked that Cowboys hat; that's why I bought it. And that's why I sometimes come down on you so hard."

All that's changed from those summer days and now is that Rod and I are interrupted much more than we ever were in Michigan. Back then, it was usually only my roommate coming home, or someone calling Rod on his cell phone.

Today, nurses are the biggest culprits. They burst into my room at the top of every hour to record my weight, blood pressure, and temperature, or to change out my empty IV bags. I have three bags now, each connected to a machine the size of a shoebox that pumps their liquids. The liquids are siphoned into a clear tube leading into a vein just below the inside of my right elbow.

The machines—I will soon have six of them, I've been told—are all attached to a pole on wheels. In the short time Rod's been here, he's twice wheeled my IV pole to the bathroom when I felt nausea or diarrhea coming on. The first time he accompanied me I was happy to have his assistance; he always waits outside till I'm done, no matter how long it takes. Yet I can't help but feel like an invalid. I've been doing things on my own for too long not to feel that way, I guess.

Once we're comfortable in our respective beds, Rod and I begin watching an old movie: *Guess Who's Coming to Dinner.*

Rod hears it's good. Real good.

"It's the first popular film to feature a black and white relationship," Rod says. "Sidney Poitier is in it. He's a great actor."

"I know," I say. "I used to see his picture on a mural on the side of a building at Sony."

The irony of this film is not lost on us.

For some of my family members visiting me—a few coming from as far away as Minnesota—seeing Rod here is like watching a scene out of *Guess Who's Coming to the Hospital Room*. There's no ill will, of course. It's just that my family is not used to being around someone of Rod's size—or color. Mom, who loves every creature on earth—as long as they're deserving of it—tells me, "I couldn't take my eyes off him when we picked him up at the airport. He's so big! I've never seen anyone like him before." And Mom's used to being around professional basketball players who have to duck their heads when they walk into her office each day.

As Rod and I settle into the movie, we're interrupted from our rest by a disturbing sound: the screeching of my hospital room door slowly opening.

A man wearing a white coat and wielding a clipboard walks in. He's young, maybe in his late 30s, and is wearing glasses. I don't recognize him as part of the "team" of doctors assigned to me: the oncologist, the intern, the fellow, the resident—six in total.

"Hello," the man says. "I'm a fertility doctor."

I roll my eyes, taking inventory of the many "specialists" that have already paraded into my room.

One doctor a couple days ago, a Korean fellow, came in and told me, "Hi, I'm Dr. So-and-so. I'm a radiologist." Then he broke down all the radiation treatments I'd be receiving in the next few weeks.

"You'll do great," he said, patting me on the shoulder. "This'll be easier than your first cancer because we won't have to do whole body radiation. Since it's just a blood disease, we can focus only on the head."

That was good news.

"Hello," another doctor said later that day. This man was old and gray. "I'm a neurologist."

I don't even know what that means.

"I'm a pathologist," another one boasted, Again, a complete mystery.

Now it seems I have a contortionist on my hands, given that this dark-haired man with spectacles suddenly morphs from a fertility doctor into a rabid football fan (keeping in mind that *fan* is short for *fanatic*) the moment he sees Rod.

"Do you play football?" the man asks after walking past my bed to Rod's cot.

I turn away, attempting to separate myself from the train wreck that will surely follow. I've witnessed people ask Rod at the most inopportune time whether he plays football. Even worse is the question that usually follows: "How much money did you make in the NFL?"

Rod immediately sits up in his cot.

"I used to play," he says without much enthusiasm.

OK, now we can get on with it: Rod has answered the question.

"What team did you play for?" the dark-haired man inquires, his eyes beaming like a seven-year-old during his first visit to Disneyland.

"Baltimore Ravens," Rod says with even less enthusiasm.

The guy *has* to get it now. Clearly, Rod is in no mood to talk about his football career.

"Is that a Super Bowl ring?" the man asks, gazing at the diamonds and multicolored stones on the large piece of jewelry resting on my nightstand.

If this were a normal, everyday situation, perhaps in a coffee shop or a sports bar, Rod might place the ring right in the fellow's hands, thus sharing with him the joy of holding such a special piece of jewelry. This is not one of those situations.

"What was it like to win the Super Bowl?" the man inquires, even though Rod has not yet answered the previous question. "When did you—?"

"Hey!" Rod barks, interrupting the guy mid-question. "The patient, is *there*."

Rod, sitting straight up in his cot, points at me. Every vein in his arm appears ready to jump out of his skin. The visitor, I notice, is stone silent, his face as ghostly white as everything else in my antiseptic hospital room. He doesn't seem to be breathing. I'm having trouble myself.

Thankfully, the tension ends as the dark-haired man slowly contorts back into a doctor.

He drops his eyes to his clipboard and starts reading through his notes, likely refreshing his memory as to why he came into my room in the first place. Finally, he starts talking fertility.

Rod, still upright, looks on intently like a chaperone at a school dance.

"You should think about freezing a sample of your sperm before they begin poking away at you. That's what Lance Armstrong did."

The doctor is smiling. He's telling me my chances of having children someday (if I make it out of here, that is) will be compromised due to the large amounts of chemotherapy I'll be receiving—and he's *smiling*?

"Too late," I tell him, adding that I've already been given enough chemotherapy and radiation in the past few days to kill a small elephant. And with all the radiation and chemo I had as a kid, the whole point is probably moot anyway. I'm likely as infertile as the day I was born.

"Oh," the man says, then drops his clipboard to his side and creeps out of the room.

Surprisingly, I'm not worried about how the hospital has devastated my chances of having a real family someday. I'm still thinking about the look on that fertility doctor's face—it was priceless—when Rod rebuked him for paying more attention to his football résumé than to me.

I don't think he'll ever make that mistake again.

CHAPTER FIVE

Those Who Stay Will Be Champions

———— ✠ ————

"Great things are not done by impulse,
but by a series of small things brought together."
—VINCENT VAN GOGH

od continues to despise the question that caused that train wreck in my hospital room; it has become a necessary evil for him. Like a movie star or famous musician who has to put up with autograph seekers and paparazzi daily, Rod has to deal with his own trials of success. He has the football career, and the gigantic Super Bowl ring, and everybody wants to know about it.

Early on, it wasn't like this.

———— ✠ ————

"I was too big to play football as a kid," Rod told me after another incidence of someone asking him at an inappropriate time whether he played football. This time we were at a restaurant, and the waiter suddenly became mesmerized by Rod's ring after he had dropped off our food.

"What do you mean 'too big'?" I asked Rod. "How can that be possible?"

"Well, my mom used to take me to tryouts at the park where we lived in Miami."

"You mean Pop Warner?"

"Yeah, peewee football, that kind of thing. The only problem Mom and I had was that I weighed as much as any kid on the 13- and 14-year-old teams, and the coaches said it wasn't fair for me to play with kids in my age group."

"How old were you?"

"About eight."

"How much did you weigh?"

"Around 140. I didn't know that was such a big deal until I learned that the average weight of a full-grown adult was 160."

"So you really couldn't play at all?"

"Nope. My mom kept thinking that 'next year' I wouldn't be as big because the other kids would have grown as big as I had. And every time we went back, it was the same."

"That must have been frustrating."

"I didn't really think about it. But yeah, I guess it was. I know my mom was frustrated. I was really rambunctious as a kid. So she was looking for something to get me involved in."

A short time after this conversation, I was preparing something to eat in my apartment when Rod's cell phone rang. He had stopped by earlier and had forgotten it then. Thinking the call might be important, I answered it.

It was Rod's mom, Linda.

"I'm sorry, but he's not here," I told her. "He left his phone at my apartment. But he should be back soon."

This was the first time I spoke to Mrs. Payne. After hearing so much about her, it was kind of a thrill. Like me, Rod talked to his mom nearly every day, so she came up a lot in conversation.

"So what have you and Rod been up to?" Mrs. Payne asked.

"He's been taking me around, introducing me to his friends. I've met a lot of them. It's been fun."

"That's good," Mrs. Payne said. "I'm worried that things are hard on Rod now. You know, now that he's not playing football anymore."

"I'm sure it is, but he seems to be handling it well. He doesn't complain about it at least. I think he's just moved on."

"Yep, that's Rod. He never gets too down on things."

"I can tell you one thing, Mrs. Payne: he's been trying to make things happen in other areas of life. We have a lot of ideas for projects and businesses and things. I used to work at Sony Pictures in LA, doing special effects for film and TV, and I still have a lot of contacts out there. Rod has some good stories for screenplays, so who knows?"

"Oh really?" Mrs. Payne said. She sounded surprised, as if she hadn't known Rod had this talent.

"Plus, he's pretty involved in the car-customizing shop he has here."

"Yes, I know about that. He's always been into cars—and motorcycles."

I didn't know about the motorcycles.

"Rod took me to the shop to meet his co-owners," I explained. "It's right here in Ann Arbor, sort of a Michigan version of MTV's *Pimp My Ride*. Do you know that show?"

"No, I don't," Mrs. Payne said with a giggle.

"They do a lot of regular business there—repair, general detail, customizing—but Rod says he's trying to get some of his former teammates to pay some good money to super-customize their cars."

"That's good to hear, because Rod needs something to keep him busy, or else he can get lost. He's easily distracted."

"It must have been hard on him when he wasn't allowed to play football as a kid."

"He told you that?"

"Yeah. But it's good that he stayed focused enough until he got a chance to play in high school."

Mrs. Payne didn't respond, so I went on.

"That was my problem; I wanted to play baseball. I was pretty good. I later won trophies in recreational softball. But in high school, I was so lost and confused I never tried out for anything. I could have played tennis, baseball, that's about it, though. I was never really good at basketball or running or anything. I was overweight as a child, so I never had any wind."

"So was Rod," Mrs. Payne said. "He even ran a little track in high school, and that helped. But he's always been overweight. He only lost that when he first started playing sports."

"How did he get involved? Did you tell him to play?"

"No. I just let him do his thing, as long as he was behaving, which wasn't always. It was hard for me, being a single parent, to take care of him. But I did it, always kept him respectful and in church, putting the Lord first."

"Yeah, he said he was a rambunctious child."

"Oh, yes, from early on."

"What happened back then? He couldn't have been that big of a problem at that young age."

"I remember being at home, sewing a wedding dress for a friend. Rod was about two. He came into the living room and asked me for a piece of cake. I'd made the cake earlier and put it on top of the refrigerator to cool. I was really into it, hemming this dress. I said, 'No, Rod, not right now. I'm trying to finish up. I'll get you some cake in a minute.' But Rod kept asking me. Finally I got frustrated and said, 'If you want it, go get it, if you think you can.'

"All of a sudden, I hear this banging noise coming from the kitchen. I got up to see what he was doing. He was standing on a chair, and he had this little push toy, the ones that go 'pop-pop-pop-pop.' He was so young, but he was swinging this thing trying to knock that cake off the fridge. He was too short to reach it, but he didn't care. He just kept swinging and swinging this big thing trying to get a piece of that cake."

"Yeah, he knows what he wants," I said, recalling the time Rod headed straight for the kitchen during his first visit to my apartment.

"It was so funny," Mrs. Payne added, "because he had no concept that if he did knock the plate off, it probably would break and he couldn't eat it anyway. I just had to stop and get him a piece of that cake, because he was *that* determined."

"Was Rod born real big?"

"No, he didn't have the body of an athlete, if that's what you mean. But he was about nine pounds. In fact, my mom and father came to the hospital when Rod was born, and they brought this cute newborn outfit. When they saw him, they turned around and went back downstairs to the gift shop to buy him something else to wear home. The outfit they had brought was too little. He couldn't wear newborn clothes."

"Did Rod have asthma when he was born? He told me about that. I don't know much about it, though. I've never seen Rod use an inhaler or anything."

"No, he's fine now. But I didn't learn he had asthma until I took him to the hospital for a fever when he was a baby. I used to take him to the hospital a lot because of fevers. This time, they put him on a bed, in a little basket with ice packed in it. And let me tell you, Steve, I couldn't believe how that bed shook. The doctor had never seen anything like it. He really started talking to me like I knew he was asthmatic, and I didn't. He said I should give Rod medications that had steroids in them. I always thought that had something to do with his size."

"So he just kept growing?"

"Yes. When Rod was five, he was already in the 80th percentile for size and height for his age."

"What does that mean?"

"Well, they had told me, the folks in his school, that anything over the 50th percentile is on the wrong side of average. And as Rod grew, his hyperactivity increased. So I took him to a doctor, who said he had ADD and prescribed Ritalin for him."

"Was that just temporary?"

"He took Ritalin every daily, I think, until I received a phone call from Rod's fourth-grade teacher."

"What did she say?"

"She told me he had done a cartwheel into class." The shock in Mrs. Payne's voice was still evident. "The teacher said she had asked Rod why he did a cartwheel into her class, and he told her he hadn't taken his pills. But Rod *had* taken his pills. He used that as an excuse. I immediately took him off the Ritalin. I didn't care what the doctors said. I started to focus on discipline instead of giving him medications. If we hadn't done that, he might have gotten into trouble later in life."

"You think so? Rod seems pretty responsible."

"You have to look at the fact that Rod was a young black man. I was trying to teach him discipline or else the police would. And I didn't like the way they would discipline him. He already had some problems because of his race when he was real young."

"What happened?"

"Well, we had moved from Orlando to a nice part of Miami shortly before I divorced Rod's father."

"So Rod was born in Orlando?"

"Yes. We moved here after Rod's father had a job transfer. Anyway, we had a big problem with a neighbor. Rod came home one day and told me that this man had told him he was not allowed in his house, because his little girl was not allowed to play with black kids. This girl was in Rod's kindergarten class, as well as his day care. It was only natural for day care kids from the same neighborhood to be friends."

"That's ridiculous," I said. "I can't even imagine that."

"See, I never wanted Rod to use race as an excuse, to think that he can't do something because he's black. I dealt with racism myself, growing up in Miami."

"I thought Rod said you were from Georgia."

"I was born there, but I grew up in Miami. And believe me there is plenty of racism here."

"So when Rod told me you were the first black female dancer in your high school, that was in Miami?"

"Yes—and cheerleader too," Mrs. Payne said, laughing. "Don't forget that."

"He didn't tell me that. That's important—can't leave that out. So what happened with that crazy neighbor?"

"I don't know. When it was time for Rod to attend high school, I took him and moved to a racially diverse neighborhood. I never thought he could have a real friendship otherwise."

"Rod said you lived in southern Miami?"

"Yes, South Miami Heights. He attended Miami Killian."

"So that's when Rod started playing football."

"Well, his first extracurricular activity was playing in the band. He had played tuba and trumpet in the band in junior high. In high school, he was supposed to be in the band, but there was some conflict with his class schedule. The only other thing open at the time was a junior varsity sport. That's how he got into sports."

"Rod said he was on the wrestling and water polo teams. But I never asked him how he got into those sports." (I had been too busy imagining Rod in the pool with all the skinny white kids.) "I thought he played those sports at the same time as football."

"Nope," Mrs. Payne says. "It was only later when Rod got into football."

"That's right. He said he didn't play until he was a junior."

"Well, it was nice talking to you, Steve. Maybe we can meet in person soon. You can come down to Florida."

"That'd be great. I'm looking forward to it. I'll tell Rod you called. I'm sure he'll be back soon. He doesn't go too far without his cell phone."

"That sounds good, Steve. You take care."

As expected, Rod dropped by a couple hours later.

"You left your phone over here," I told him as he charged through the door. "Were you looking for it? Your mom called. I talked to her for a while."

"Oh yeah? What'd she have to say?"

"She just wanted to know what's going on. We talked a little bit about your childhood. I told her it was kind of similar to mine, except for the football part. She told me that you played those other sports in high school before football. How did you start playing football? You got sick of wrestling and water polo?"

"No, I kept playing those sports. But right before my junior year I was at a barbershop, Moss Barber Shop in Miami, and ran into Sam Miller—that's my high school coach. He was coaching at another high school at the time. He got me to play."

"Did you know him?"

"No, but we got to talking, and he said he was transferring to Killian."

"So you just went out to practice?"

"Yeah. At first I didn't know if I wanted to play. I knew I had the physical gifts needed to help the team, but I didn't think I was going to do it. I'd never played before."

"What got you to play?"

"My coach talked to me and said if I could play, then I'd end up learning things about myself that I couldn't learn in a textbook, or even playing other sports. Football is different, he said. It's the ultimate team game, and it would help me find out things I wasn't willing to admit I was looking for, like a lot of kids my age from that part of Miami. I saw some crazy things around that time."

"Like what?"

"Just people, friends of mine, running drugs, doing stupid stuff just for pocket change. It wasn't that bad of a neighborhood, but you had to know how to handle yourself."

"So what were you looking for?"

"A father to come home to every day, mostly. Not having one left an emptiness inside me. I had no one to look up to, no one to emulate. No hero."

"Yeah, but you showed him. You played football for just two years and became a Division I recruit."

"Yup," Rod said nonchalantly. "I just took to it."

"So you didn't see your dad at all?"

"Oh, there were weekend visits where I heard about the basics of life, like how to shoot a gun or always make sure you have a condom on hand. But past that, nothing."

"Looks like our dads were pretty different. My dad wouldn't even think about bringing up those subjects, girls or guns. Not until I was older, at least, when I already knew what I knew. Then he'd get all aggravated that I wouldn't listen to him. I wasn't doing it on purpose: it was just natural. I was already grown up. I needed a friend more than a father."

"That's where I was lucky," Rod said. "I had my coaches come in and teach me what my mom couldn't give me and what my dad didn't offer me."

⇥◆⇤

Jamie Morris is right: unless you're a Michigan graduate—or just a huge Michigan football fan—you don't follow the Wolverines or any other team in the Big Ten Conference much if you grew up in Los Angeles.

Where I'm from, Pac-10 football is king—UCLA, USC, Arizona State. That's all you ever hear about—the Bruins, Trojans, Sun Devils.

Of course, everything changed when I became a student at Michigan.

The first thing I learned is that *all* Michigan football games are unforgettable experiences, not just the rivalry games: the Michigan States; the Ohio States; the nonconference, national TV games against Florida State and Notre Dame.

This is because there hasn't been a crowd at Michigan Stadium of fewer than 100,000 in more than 30 years. I remember going to a football game at my community college in LA. It was on a Friday afternoon, and I could literally count the fans in attendance: 52.

Roughly a year later, during my first Michigan football game—against Eastern Michigan University, from down the road in Ypsilanti—I got chills when I heard Howard King, Michigan's longtime public address announcer, say, "You are part of the largest crowd to be watching a football game in America today." What a feeling to hear those words ring out in that stadium, a legion of maize-and-blue-clad fans around me on a breezy, colorful afternoon, the Midwest sky so perfect.

After meeting Rod, I know those games would have been even more amazing if I had seen him play in them. I can hear King's unmistakable baritone voice now: "At center . . . a senior co-captain from Miami, Florida . . . Number 52 . . . *Rod Paaaayyynne!*"

Imagining everything that Rod accomplished at Michigan, I found it interesting to learn he almost never made it to Ann Arbor.

"I was recruited to Florida, Florida State, Miami, South Carolina, Tennessee, UCLA," Rod told me, after I asked him how he chose Michigan.

"Was there more?"

"Oh yeah. I got letters from all over. And a lot of head coaches of those teams came to our house. I remember Pat Dye, the old coach of Auburn. He sat right on my mom's couch. 'Ma'am'"—Rod used a deep Southern drawl, which he pulled off to a T—"'He'll get a good education. Yo' boy'll get a goooood education if he comes to Auburn.'"

"Did Lloyd Carr come to your house?"

"No. Cam Cameron, my offensive coordinator—he's with the San Diego Chargers now—he recruited me. Cam had a heck of a time at my house though."

"What do you mean?"

"As I was walking him to his car, some shots rang out."

"No way."

"Yep. Cam hit the deck and started shouting, 'What's that? What's that?' Our neighbor across the street was shooting at someone breaking into his truck. I yelled, 'Stop acting like an idiot.' That probably made my neighborhood look pretty bad."

"Probably. But it didn't matter, right? Michigan wanted you."

"Yep, but I was upset with them."

"Why?"

"I played tackle, and my high school coach said I'd be an All-America guard in college. That's what I wanted. But when I got to Michigan, they put me at center in the first practice. I didn't want to play center. Then a month after I got there, Hurricane Andrew hit Florida."

"I remember that. Was it pretty bad?"

"Put it this way, everyone I knew, my grandparents, aunts and uncles, friends, former teammates, coaches, all could have used my help cleaning up after the storm. My mom's house was blown away. She had to stay for months in a hotel in Fort Lauderdale.

"She rebuilt the house in the same spot. I remember I wanted to leave Michigan so I could go home and take care of her. But she made me stay. She said there was a reason I went to Michigan and that I had to put my heart in it."

"So was it hard getting acclimated at center?"

"Yeah, because you have to do it all at center. Nothing starts without you. You have to read the defenses, check off plays. Plus, you do more banging than any other position because you're right in the middle of the front line. But I had to step it up. I was just one of 15 players on my high school football team to receive a Division I-A scholarship. Heck, I was just the 40th-best college prospect in Florida. So I had something to prove."

"So did you fit in right away at Michigan?" I asked Rod. "I remember after I visited the campus for the first time, I felt this sense of belonging. That made it easier for me."

"Yeah, it was pretty much the same for me. When I flew into Detroit and then saw this campus, I knew there was something different about this place. You have to remember, I had never been north of the Mason Dixon Line before. When your family lives in Florida and comes from Georgia, there's no reason to."

"Did you take all five recruiting visits?" The NCAA allows five trips to schools. Any more is a violation.

"I did, but none of them compared to Michigan. I didn't know all the stories and everything that Michigan was at the time, but it just seemed like what a college should be. They took all of the recruits to the Fab Five game, when Michigan lost to Duke in overtime. The atmosphere was amazing."

The Fab Five, I knew, was the trash-talking group of freshmen hoopsters led by Chris Webber, Jalen Rose, and Juwan Howard (all longtime NBA stars). They're as notorious in college basketball as the Detroit Pistons' Bad Boys of the NBA.

"We sat courtside at Crisler Arena, and I'll never forget Bobby Hurley slamming his hands on the court right before tip-off—he was so hyped up."

"What's it like to be a D-I recruit? Is it pure excitement all the time, the minute you get to campus?"

"A little. I mean, I thought I was the man of the hour. I was the proverbial know-it-all freshman. 'Yeah, yeah! I'm Rod Payne. Where's my jersey? Who are you? Don't matter; I'll take you on. Just let me at the field. *Where's the damn field?*'"

"No kidding?" I could picture Rod at that time, saying those things.

"I was a dawg," Rod added, "ready to gnarl at anyone and gnaw on any fresh meat thrown my way. Argggghhh!"

"That's amazing."

"Yeah. The thing is, guys with an attitude like that don't last very long at Michigan. I had to learn my lessons the hard way. I ain't gonna lie to you, there were some practices when I was crying. I was calling my mom, wanting to come home. But she said to stick it out or I'd regret it later. That's where God really began working in my life. I trusted him to carry me through those days, to get up each day and go back to the field. It was hard to humble myself and know the coaches were right, that I just wasn't playing with the right attitude."

"So you changed your attitude and became captain?"

"It wasn't that easy. Captain is the most prestigious honor you can get at Michigan because the players vote for it. That's your teammates saying, '*You* lead us.' I'll put it to you this way: it took a lot of toiling, grinding out—pruning out—all that arrogant attitude before guys could gain any respect or rise to any prominence within the structure of the team. And it usually started in practice, not in the games with all the TV cameras and pomp and circumstance."

"Were those intense, the practices?"

"At the end of some workouts, it was all about heart. And that's where players are born."

"Can you give me an example?"

"OK. They have this rope, 25 or 30 yards of rope, three inches thick, with a loop at the end. What happens is, a coach has the rope around his waste—sometimes he's the assistant strength and conditioning coach—and he stands against a wall. You—imagine you're a player doing this drill—you pull one hand over the other until you can pull the guy past a line. It should take a strong guy three to seven minutes to pull a guy in—the coach knows when to resist. When you start, you can pull him hard for five to 10 yards. No matter how hard a coach resisted, I could snatch him off his feet. But most guys' muscles were torn 'cause it was the end of practice."

"I watched this one kid from Ypsilanti," Rod continued. "He was falling on the ground, spitting. I watched this 18-year-old freshman for darn near 20 minutes, falling on the ground, darn near in tears. There was a weight room full of guys around him telling him 'This is what Michigan football is like.' We didn't mess with the guy. 'Get it going,' we told him, slapping him on the back. 'Get on your feet.' This guy was fighting tooth and nail. Not too many people know what it's like to soldier on when you're at the point of exhaustion.

"You could see he was struggling. And when that struggle turned into a pure hatred, that was the only thing that brought him all the way in. For the guys that don't go to that extreme, who try to just skate through it—"

Rod didn't finish the sentence, but I could guess what he meant: you had to prove yourself, no matter who you were.

"The reporters were writing about them like they were going to be the greatest thing at Michigan. And then they never even made it to the first game of the season."

"Is that what 'Those who stay will be champions' means?" I asked, knowing it was the slogan former Michigan head coach, Bo Schembechler, had come up with. (There are T-shirts in the stores with that saying on it.)

"Sure is. Bo used those words to describe the player who earns everything the Michigan football program has to offer," Rod said.

"What's that?"

"Character, discipline, pride, success—on and off the field."

"You did stay, didn't you?"

"I did, and I became Michigan's 12th All-American center. That's the best center in the country—voted on by the coaches, not the media—after being the 40th-best prospect in Florida. That shows you the power of a team environment, if it's well run."

Rod told me about a letter he received from former U.S. president Gerald Ford, who was another center at Michigan.

"Class of 1935," Rod said. "He used to come back to Ann Arbor to rally the troops every few years."

"What'd the letter say?"

"He just thanked me for my leadership and contributions to the Michigan football program, for carrying on the tradition of success."

"Where's the letter now?"

"I have it in a trunk over at Brent's, the buddy I've been staying with in Chelsea. He's actually like my godfather. I'm part of his family. I keep all of my awards and stuff in that trunk. Some things are back in Miami, though, at my mom's place."

"You should put them up somewhere," I suggested. "Like a trophy case."

"No. In football, the rewards come from what you do on the field, and in the locker room, and after you graduate. Football is not the glorified sport people think it is. It can be, but only after so much work and after so much has been sacrificed. And that's where Bo left the legacy with 'Those who stay will be champions.' It's not 'Those who arrive . . .'"

CHAPTER SIX

How Are My Patients?

—⟨⬦⟩—

"Experience is not what happens to a man;
it is what a man does with what happens to him."
—Aldous Huxley

od and I are groggy from a sleepless night in the hospital when an overly cheery nurse bursts into the room.

"How are my patients today?" she asks as she marches past my bed and Rod's cot to the window. Before getting her answer, the nurse grabs hold of the curtains and, in one motion, whips them to each side, allowing a piercing, merciless sun to flood the room.

Rod and I dive under our sheets.

We're still fuming at the orderly who came into the room at the top of every hour throughout the night to take my vitals. Now, as if this wake-up call isn't enough at this ghastly hour—around 7 a.m.—the nurse proceeds to kick up the tension a few more notches by posing yet another question.

Noticing the giant University of Michigan flag on the wall behind my bed—dark blue with a yellow block *M* in the middle—she asks, "Oh, is that Michigan State?"

Rod and I shoot up in our beds. We stare at each other in disbelief. Michigan State? Did she say that? No, she couldn't have.

"Do you see an *S* on that flag?" we ask the lady, practically in unison. "Do you see any green on it?"

The nurse shrugs her shoulders, revealing to us her blatant lack of a proper college football education. As she hands me a Dixie cup full of my morning pills (my new Lucky Charms, a mixture of red pills, greens ones, blues ones—magically delicious!), I attempt to point out her error.

"Michigan State? That'd be like asking a UCLA fan if he has a USC flag on the wall," I say.

She *has* to understand that. I mean, we're in Southern California. Apparently not, as she just shoots me a blank look.

"They're enemies!" I bark, in genuine Rod style. "Archrivals. UCLA and USC don't get along. Get it?"

Still the blank look.

"Michigan and Michigan State are rivals."

"Oh," she says as she takes back her Dixie cup. (She has me so frazzled I nearly choke on one of the marshmallowy shapes.) The nurse offers no more words. Instead, she just flushes my IV line with Saline saltwater to get the air bubbles out.

"Man, she don't understand," Rod says, falling back into his cot with a thump. I follow his lead.

While struggling to fall back asleep, I think about the question the nurse just asked us. Not about the flag, but the one before it: how are we doing this morning?

The nurse used the word *patients*—plural—while greeting us. It seemed instinctive. She doesn't know anything about Michigan sports—or sports at all, for that matter—but she knows Rod and I are a team. That is how it always was back in Michigan.

—◄══►—

Following our second serendipitous meeting, Rod and I became nearly inseparable. The bond we forged was helped along by a story I wrote about him for the *Ann Arbor News*.

When I approached my editors about doing the story, I became nervous. They'd shot down a few of my story ideas before, so I was thinking they might do it again. (I was still relatively new at the paper and didn't have much clout. I think that was the reason for the rejections.) But my editors happened to jump on this idea. So quickly, in fact, they never bothered to ask how I got the scoop. That was when I started to understand the scope of Rod's popularity.

Before I interviewed Rod, I began researching some of the old articles written about him.

A quick Internet search revealed he'd been featured prominently in all the state publications—lead stories in the *Detroit News* and *Free Press* (its Sunday edition, when the papers combine), and the *Ann Arbor News*. He was also in national periodicals. Rod was quoted in *Sports Illustrated* after a tough loss to Penn State. He gave the higher-ranked Nittany Lions credit for their victory, claiming they were the best team in the nation. I found his humility impressive.

I also found, while searching through the overflowing bookshelves in the *News'* sports department, a Michigan football game day program with Rod on the cover. On another shelf, jammed between some Michigan football media guides of years past, I spotted a dusty copy of the *Wolverine*.

Published once a week during the school year, the *Wolverine* is a tabloid-sized newspaper featuring only University of Michigan sports. This one, dated November 6, 1995 (Rod's junior year), featured a full-color cover photo of Rod snapping the ball with three fingers on his left hand wrapped in tape and splints. The headline—PLAYING WITH PAYNE: Laughter Stops When Comic Rod Payne Hits the Field—is followed by a secondary headline inside: NO PAYNE, NO GAIN: Rod Payne Reigns As U–M's Humorous Hard-Guy.

Jon Borton, senior staff writer at the *Wolverine*, started his article by highlighting Rod's ability to take abuse on the field. He listed many of Rod's poundings over the years—"busted wrist, surgically repaired shoulder, a foot that once swelled up like a bowling ball." The article also included comments from Rod's coaches and teammates. The coaches critiqued his play on the field, while his teammates ribbed him like only teammates do.

"He thinks he's the only one who can block me," lamented Jarrett Irons, Rod's future co-captain. "We have a competition between us, and I get the better of him every time."

"Me and Jarrett are really competitive," Rod responded in the article. "If he gets whacked on a play, man, I'm laughin'; I'm rollin'. My guts are falling out."

Lloyd Carr, for his part, had nothing but glowing remarks about his future MVP.

"Rod Payne is my kind of football player," he said. "He plays with great emotion, he loves the game, he's smart, and I think he's one of the more gifted football players we've had at Michigan. . . . He came out [against Northwestern] last week with a broken bone in his hand. He never even considered that he wouldn't play. He's played with a bad foot. He's played with serious injuries that a lot of guys are going to say, 'I can't play.' . . . He is mentally and physically a very tough individual."

Carr also said this about Rod: "I think before he's done, he's going to have one of the great careers at Michigan."

With more than enough information for my story, I made out a list of questions and scheduled my interview with Rod.

It began around 11 p.m. one weekday in my apartment. Rod shared with me his reaction after Cincinnati selected him with its first pick in the third round of the 1997 NFL Draft.

"I was the second center chosen, so I was excited," Rod told me as *SportsCenter* played at low volume in the background. "But after I was drafted, my agent called and said, 'I have good and bad news. The bad news is you've been drafted by Cincinnati. The good news is it can only get better.'"

I found it odd that Rod's agent would have said that. Sure the Cincinnati Bengals were the laughingstock of football at the time, but they were in the NFL. That should have been reason to celebrate.

"What did you think about going to the Bengals?"

"When they signed me, I thought it was going to be like it was at Michigan. I thought it would be an extension of the pride and dedication and teamwork I experienced there. I was so excited to be a Bengal that I used my signing-bonus money to buy a house in Cincinnati. My agent told me that wasn't a good idea, but I didn't listen to him."

"Why was that a bad idea?"

"He thought it would take away our leverage during contract negotiations. But I didn't care. I told him just to lock up the contract so I could get started."

"Were you already hurt when you got drafted?" I remembered Borton's article said Rod's dislocated shoulder had "popped out so many times" during his sophomore season that it required surgery after the bowl game.

"I just had that one surgery in college because it kept lingering," Rod said. "Other than that, I was ready to go."

"So the injuries were the biggest reason things didn't go well in Cincinnati?"

"Along with how bad the Bengals were," Rod bemoaned. "Do you know I lost more games in my second year playing with Cincinnati than during my entire career at Michigan?"

"Really?"

"We won three games that year, in 1998. That's 13 games we lost that year. Add up all my losses at Michigan, and it's not as many as that."

For the next hour, in-between trips to the kitchen for chips and soda, Rod talked more about his frustrating years with the Bengals. He would often speak tongue-in-cheek about them, but I could tell deep down they tore him apart.

"My three years in Cincinnati were so bad," Rod said, "a radio station paid for a plane to fly around our practice field for an hour dragging a sign that said, 'Fire Bruce Coslet.'"

Coslet, the Bengals' head coach, was in his second year at the time. He eventually resigned three games into the 2000 season.

"It was so bad," Rod continued, "I would drive up Interstate 71 to my house, every day after practice darn near in tears, debating whether to quit football. Honestly, there was a point while playing for the Bengals when I said, 'Man, forget this!' I'd rather have never played pro football than play on that team. And you know what? That was the general consensus of the entire team."

"So when did you get traded to the Ravens?"

"I wasn't traded. Before my third year, I was preparing to have dual knee surgeries—it was before the start of the 1999 season—and the Bengals released me."

"I thought you could only be released if you were a bad player or got into trouble."

"You're right—they're not supposed to release you. They knew I was injured. They should have done something about it, like put me on injured reserve."

"What happened after that?"

"I filed a grievance with the NFL Players' Union. It was settled, but the whole thing made me feel like I was in a black hole. I did start getting offers from other teams, but there's so much stupid stuff that goes on."

That thought caused Rod to shift positions on the couch. He seemed perturbed.

"What teams called?"

"Let's see . . . Kansas City. I went and worked out for them, but they red-flagged me on the physical. Then I went to Denver; they red-flagged me too. After that workout—it was so cold there, my whole body ached—I went to the hotel, sat down on the edge of my bed, and rubbed my knees. I held my head in my hands. I knew I was really hurt. I did those workouts knowing that I had two jacked-up knees. I called my agent the next day and told him not to schedule any more workouts."

"What happened next?"

"Here's how insane it was: I had to have two knee surgeries— I messed up one in a preseason game against Indy, and the other one was messed up before that. Instead of having one surgery and taking five months off and then having another one, I did both at the same time. The surgeon took two hours in between surgeries. I pushed it, but I was ready to go in April for spring practice."

"So how did you get hooked up with the Ravens?"

"They always wanted me," Rod said, his voice perking up. "They had wanted me since I came out of school. They were actually one of the teams who had worked me out after the Bengals and had also red-flagged me. But my offensive line coach in Baltimore, Jim Colletto, was head coach at Purdue when I was playing at Michigan. He knew what kind of player I was. He knew the Michigan staff too. So I think he was really high on me. So after the Ravens brought me in, I saw their doctor in April 2000. They tested me and said I was ready to go."

"So did you play in the preseason?"

"Oh yeah, I played in 80 percent of the offensive plays in the preseason games. A lot of people don't know this, but we were the only team in the NFL to win all four preseason games that year."

"That's pretty cool. So what happened then?"

"Everything was good, but I knew I wasn't the player I used to be." Rod rubbed his knees, and I could see the scars twisting across them like rivers on a map. "I spent the whole off-season working out, getting back in shape. I went to training camp and did good, but I was still hurt. I realized that surgery never repairs you the same. It can help you play again, but the fix rarely is permanent. It buys you time, then it creeps back. I had so many things I played through. I had to take pain medications. . . ."

Rod's voice trailed off, no longer the trumpeting vessel it was at the start of the interview.

"Billick," Rod said, referring to Ravens head coach, Brian Billick, "brought me in and said, 'Rod, we're releasing you. We have a situation with a hurt tackle, and we're in more dire need for a backup tackle than we are a backup center.'

"Colletto, who loves me, saw that I wasn't the player I was in college and told me I should retire. He said, 'Whatever you do, you will be the best. You are great.'"

"So how did you end up back on the team?"

"Thing is, Billick knew I was still a good player. I wasn't the same, but I could still help the team. Before I left camp, he said, 'Rod, stay in shape, because I have a feeling you will be back on this team.'"

The enthusiasm in Rod's voice picked up again.

"I missed the whole first half of the season, but sure as heck they called me. Billick called. He asked, 'You in shape, ready to go?' I flew in and took a physical. I was supposed to go pheasant hunting in Michigan when he called.

"It was great," Rod added, his voice returned to its dominant form. "This is how close the Ravens are, how Billick made guys pull together. When I walked into the locker room, I got my old locker and uniform from the equipment guy, and then it was nothing but love out on the field. Practice was just ending, and all the guys came up to me saying, 'Hey, Rod. How you doing? Welcome back.' And Billick walked up to me and said, 'Rod, I told you you'd be back here.' I shook hands with him and said, 'Coach, I respect you as a man of your word. Now let me get on my uniform and get to work.'"

"I wasn't fooled," Rod added. "They needed insurance, a quality backup in case one of their guys went down. And that was cool with me. If I wasn't healthy, I was comfortable doing spot duty. I worked hard, studied defenses, and helped out in the locker room."

"Who cares what your capacity was?" I said. "You were on the team. You won it all."

"Yeah, and the funny thing is, Baltimore never lost again after I joined the team," Rod told me, smiling. "They were 5-4 at the time, and we won the final 11 games."

"I'll bet that made up for a lot that happened in Cincinnati."

"Oh, definitely," Rod said. "Things were so bad there, I can't even believe it. You want to hear a story? I don't know how much you need for your article.

"It was our last game of the 1998 season, against Tampa Bay." Rod was still going strong at nearly 3 a.m. "It was two days after Christmas, and if we beat Tampa Bay, Tampa Bay doesn't go to the playoffs. So we could be a spoiler. And Tampa Bay whooped our butts—35 to nothing.

Thirty-five-zip! And you know what? I came out of our locker room after the game, and 70 percent—no, that's too low of a number. I'm willing to bet 85 percent of the guys on the team were not even in the state anymore."

"What do you mean 'not in the state'?"

"They had their possessions with them in U-Hauls, on a plane, boat, car . . . you name it, before the game so they could leave right when the game was over. Our last game was over at four o'clock, and by eight o'clock there couldn't have been more than a handful of players with us. The rest of them were already wherever it was they were going."

"You know what?" Rod said, after a long pause, "forget them for not knowing what a true football player, a truly dedicated team player, is all about. Forget the Bengals for not harboring the number of guys that come in there and want to be different. They draft great talent, guys off winning college teams. They always have the number one or two or three pick in the draft. Forget them for not cultivating that talent, for keeping those cancerous players."

"'Cancerous' players?"

"When I got to Cincinnati in 1997, on a 58-man team—53 plus five practice squad players—ready to go on Day One of the regular season, I would say that 10 to 15 guys, by themselves, were enough to bring down a group of players. That means if you have a guy sitting at running back with a bad attitude, a selfish attitude, he's a cancerous player. He can literally turn a group of running backs in the room by destroying their morale. He can turn that room from a good room into a bad room, just that one guy."

That part sunk in. Not because Rod referred to the saboteurs as cancers, but because of how incorrigible their actions were, how detrimental to the team (which is all that matters, I gathered from listening to Rod) they really were.

Soon, the interview slowed to a halt.

It was a little after 4 a.m. Late enough, apparently, for Rod to ask if he could crash out on the couch, the one he'd been dropping potato chip crumbs on the last four or five hours.

Chelsea, where Rod was staying, was at least a half-hour drive away—maybe 20 minutes at that late hour, but still far enough to be a pain. I knew this from having covered high school golf tournaments there.

"Sure. Let me get you a blanket," I said.

Realizing I didn't have one, I fetched the comforter off my bed.

"Here," I said. "With the pillows from the couch, you'll be fine."

⊷ ⊷ ⊷ ⊷

Rod swept the chips off the couch, scooped them into his hand, and headed to the garbage can.

"You now know 99 percent more than most reporters do," he said, his voice trailing off as he turned the corner into the kitchen.

That immediately sunk in. In just a few hours, I'd gone from a neophyte journalist to a place nary a sportswriter goes—inside the world of a professional athlete. This was all thanks to my MVP guest, who had been to the mountaintop and had come back down to talk about it.

Why I was so lucky I could only wonder as I drifted off asleep, just before sunrise.

CHAPTER SEVEN

Unannounced Arrival

"I found out that if you are going to win games,
you had better be ready to adapt."
—Scotty Bowman

I woke up the day after my interview with Rod (or rather later that day), and as I yawned away the sleep, I thought about everything Rod had told me those few hours earlier. We had talked about so much, yet I was able to fully digest it in the short time I slept. I knew this because, when I opened my eyes, I wasn't thinking about my next story.

I'd been doing that, without fail, since longer than I wished to remember. Somewhere along the line, I figured this was the price I had to pay to become the best sportswriter ever (or at least among the best, which would be fine with me).

Realizing my thoughts were taking me down a road I didn't want to go at that early hour—11 a.m.—I decided to get my day started. I was thinking way too much, spoiling the good feeling I had had when I woke up, a feeling I hadn't had 24 hours earlier, when I still didn't know as much as my fellow sportswriters: writers with a decade or two of experience on me, columnists at major newspapers, guests on national television sports shows, annual award-winners. And most important, writers with respect from their peers.

"Did you read Wilbon's column today?" the guys on the *News'* overnight desk often asked me. "How about that Plaschke piece? Amazing. You should check it out, Rom. You might learn something."

Our paper ran columns from these modern-day sportswriting legends—Michael Wilbon of the *Washington Post* and Bill Plaschke of the *Los Angeles Times*, both of whom now have successful shows on ESPN. The overnight guys, who designed the sports section, came across their columns on the Associated Press wire while searching for breaking news to get into the following afternoon's edition.

That was all I'd ever wanted: a fair shake from my peers, for someone to see my potential and say to another young reporter someday, "Did you read Rom's column? Amazing."

As the late-morning sun shone through my bedroom blinds, I noticed again that my thoughts were going astray. I immediately refocused on my interview with Rod.

I thought about how devastating it must be for a football player to have major surgery. Rod, I'm sure, would still be playing in the NFL if there were even a ghost of a chance he could. He said the Jacksonville Jaguars offered him $425,000 to play as their backup center after his lone season in Baltimore. Taking the offer would have meant Rod could be closer to home, to his mother, and to all of his extended family members. But none of that mattered; he just couldn't do it.

"I wanted to be able to walk again someday," Rod had told me.

Rod also told me there were times when he couldn't fly home after games unless he shot his knees full of cortisone. Only then could he join his fellow linemen in the back of the plane. Sometimes, he couldn't even play in the games without the shots.

"That's the essence of football," Rod said. "People think it's a spectator sport, a hundred thousand people around you. But when those guys walk onto that field, and you're this close from your opponent's face [he spread his index finger and thumb about five inches apart], you think I'm thinking about that fanfare? Heck no. It's about me and you, mano a mano, and that's the essence of it."

"That's what makes football players so dangerous in other areas of their lives," Rod surmised, "because they're so used to sucking it up and pressing through pain. It's sort of like being a soldier."

Replaying those words in my mind, I was ready to face the day. That meant it was time to get out of bed and see what Rod was doing. I walked down the hallway to the living room. After passing the kitchen and turning the corner, I discovered Rod was nowhere to be found. The comforter was there, strewn halfway across the couch and the floor, and the front door was closed but unlocked. I laughed just wondering whether Rod had been kidnapped, but I knew he had probably let himself out because he had things to do.

As for me, that was hardly the case.

My daily routine had become as mundane and choreographed as a bad TV sitcom: I worked late at the office most nights, so I slept in the next morning. For the next half hour or more after waking, I wrestled to get out of bed. From there, I would fix myself a bowl of cereal and find a spot on the couch next to Arun and watch back-to-back reruns of *Wings*, his favorite show, though I have no idea why. After wolfing down the cereal and tossing the bowl into the cluttered sink—neither of us did dishes very often—I would go back to my bedroom, sit at my desk, and work on stories for the paper while wearing the clothes I slept in.

Eventually, I'd muster the energy to shower, get dressed, and walk to campus to do my errands. As a bonus, I might stop at the arcade on South University Avenue, drop a couple quarters into the classics— Centipede, Pole Position, Ms. Pac-Man—thus connecting with the happier times of my youth. I've always been very good at video games.

Somehow, with what little I accomplished during the day, the hours seemed to go by in record time. Before I knew it, evening would beckon me to the *Ann Arbor News*' three-story downtown building.

Once logged into my computer in the buzzing sports department (even at night, it had a certain pulse), I divvied up my time answering phones, completing the stories I started earlier, and quite often, peering through one of the top-floor windows at the streets below.

I would stare—angry at times, though at nothing in particular—at downtown Ann Arbor. Yet in my mind's eye I was looking over Times Square.

I can really play tricks with my head. It comes, I think, from a childhood of watching movies, digesting Hollywood story lines, and pretending they're happening to me. It would get to where I felt I really was peering onto West 43rd Street from atop the *New York Times'* high-rise. Or maybe I'd be looking at Broadway Boulevard from the third floor of the *Los Angeles Times'* downtown building, where its sports department resides.

Some *Times* . . . somewhere, soon! I cried out from inside.

Despite my vast opportunities to learn the journalism business in Ann Arbor, the respect I craved simply couldn't be found there.

I saw the attention I got from athletes and their coaches when I would freelance for other papers, major papers—the *Baltimore Sun*, *Denver Post*, and others. They gave me a little extra attention, and more respect, than when I was just a reporter with the *Ann Arbor News*.

I did that almost every night—peer out the window of the newsroom and envision the day I'd be working for one of those major metropolitan papers. I think my aims were transparent to my coworkers, like they could actually hear the turncoat thoughts stirring in my head. I can think of no other reason they never really welcomed me into their clique.

One of them, to my shock, didn't even invite me to his wedding, even though most of the sports staff went. (I heard them talking about it the next day in the newsroom.) Still, this exclusion didn't seem to bother me as much as it should have.

I had never been accepted by my peers anyway, so I was hardly in a shambles over the wedding snub. Most of my coworkers, I knew, were probably jealous because I had received a promotion after just a few months on the job, while they'd been working at the paper for years and were still covering high school synchronized swimming: the most "mind-numbing" sport you can cover at the paper, one coworker told me. Frankly, I was too focused on my goal—making it beyond the *Ann*

Arbor News—to worry about being on the outs with my coworkers.

I think Rod recognized my lofty goals as well, which is why he spent so much time with me.

Rod showed up at 1313 nearly every day, usually after working out across the street at Schembechler Hall. When he arrived, the routine was always the same.

"What's up, bro?" he would ask as I greeted him at the door. Rod would then proceed to make himself at home—usually by making a beeline for the kitchen.

One thing I found astounding about Rod's impromptu arrivals is how he could always locate a morsel of food in the kitchen I didn't even know we had—such as the can of clam chowder from way in the back of the floor-level cupboard during his first visit after the VIP party. He just seemed so resourceful that day, so confident. I liked him from the start—not the myth I'd heard so much about, but the man.

Rod arrived for the second part of our interview later the day of our first Q&A session. As usual, there was no call, no advance warning. Rod just showed up when he wanted to talk.

This time, before Rod slipped past me, I announced I had to be at work soon. It didn't seem to shake him.

"What time do you get off?" he asked.

"Around midnight," I replied, though I had to think about it. Usually, I left the office when the work was done, no sooner, no later.

"No problem," Rod said. "I'll be back."

Rod didn't specify exactly *when* he would be back, so I made it a point to arrive home a little early that night, around 11:45. Sure enough, the knock on the door arrived soon after.

This time when I opened the door, Rod slid by me. He offered the customary "What's happening?" and a pat on the shoulder, then made his way to what was becoming his regular spot on the living room couch.

"You have anything to eat?" he asked.

"I don't know," I said, still marveling at his entrance. (Kramer from *Seinfeld* has nothing on Rod.) "You ate all of the chips last night."

We skipped the hors d'oeuvres and commenced Round 2 of our interview. I had a fresh stack of mini cassettes for my tape recorder, and I was showing no sign of tiring after the long night at work.

Rod started by peppering me with stories and insights on football at all levels, high school, college, the pros. I slam-dunked the questions I prepared prior to our interview into the trash. Rod was the perfect interview: as soon as the tape started rolling, he started talking. (I read in one of the old *Detroit Free Press* articles that Rod fancies himself the "Mouth of the South," an homage to Jimmy Hart of the old World Wrestling Federation.)

One story Rod told me—of the off-the-field variety—was about a famous comedian who performed a stand-up show for a large gathering of current and former Michigan football players. While on stage, he made a player in the audience the butt of too many jokes.

"I wasn't there," Rod said, "but I heard he was upset about all these jokes, so he took a full can of beer and threw it at the comedian. Split his head in two!"

My jaw hit the floor.

"Blood went everywhere!" Rod continued.

"Why'd he get so angry? Didn't he expect that kind of thing could happen at a comedy show?"

"I heard some of the guys tried to calm him down. He said he just got crazy because he didn't like being made fun of. You know, I actually ran into that comedian since that happened."

"No way. Did you say anything to him?"

"I noticed the stitches in his forehead. I was like, 'Wow, how's that doing?' He said, 'Man, I'm *never* working for football players again. You guys are crazy.'"

As Rod and I wound down our second interview—it ended a little earlier than the previous day, around 3 a.m.—I started to believe he and I were the reincarnation of Howard Cosell and Muhammad Ali.

It seemed I was finally getting that respect I craved.

After Rod left—he was comfortable driving home this time—I turned on the TV and caught some of the early morning *SportsCenter*. As I did, I wondered whether I then knew 99.9 percent more than my fellow sports reporters.

CHAPTER EIGHT

The Token Friend

"I was taught to feel, perhaps too much,
the self-sufficient power of solitude.
—WILLIAM WORDSWORTH

After my interviews with Rod were complete, I took on the task of transcribing the tapes and writing his story.

Three days and a half-dozen Starbucks lattes later, I had seven pages of single-spaced notes with the acronym OTR noted at least three or four times on each page. Those were to remind me of what Rod instructed I keep off the record, such as the story about the comedian and the loaded beer can.

I worked a little each day on the story, juggling it with the rest of my duties at the newspaper. Meanwhile, Rod continued to drop by my apartment. His visits prolonged the writing process because we kept going over new information, and, of course, took all those necessary breaks.

Sometimes we'd go to a campus bar for lunch and grab a burger and a beer. Or we'd meet up with Rod's friends at one of their houses. We might also break away and go to a movie, the mall, or a restaurant—anywhere the mood dictated.

One afternoon, Rod told me we were taking a trip to Chelsea so he could introduce me to the family he'd been staying with since he retired, the Ecklers. Rod said Brent Eckler, the patriarch, was a longtime supporter of the Michigan football program.

"I met him my freshman year. He knew I didn't have any family of my own nearby—other than my Michigan family—so he started inviting me over for home-cooked meals."

Brent, along with his wife, Lori, and two children live in a three-story house with 10 acres of farmland.

"I used to spend a lot of time out here," Rod said, as we walked up the driveway.

"I can see why," I thought as I sucked in the country air.

From the moment I met Brent and his family, I could tell how Rod became so close to them. They embraced me like they did Rod all of those years ago.

"Hi. It's so nice to meet you," Mrs. Eckler said as I stepped into the house, a spacious abode with oak decor and plenty of small-town charm. "Rod's told me so much about you."

"Thank you. It's nice to meet you too."

"So you're from LA. But you went to school at Michigan?"

"Yes," I told Mrs. Eckler. "I was turned down from UCLA, where I first wanted to go. But that turned out to be a good thing."

"I'm sure. Michigan is a great school," she said.

"All except for the football team," Brent quipped, having just walked into the kitchen, where we'd gathered. He was looking at Rod.

"Forget you, man," Rod said, laughing while he poured a glass of lemonade.

As Rod drank the lemonade and began stockpiling Mrs. Eckler's fresh-baked cookies, I talked a little with Brent.

"I'm a former baseball player," he said.

"Baseball? Not football?"

"No way. I was always too small."

"So how'd you meet Rod?" I asked Brent, who didn't look all that small to me.

"We met when he came over to my house to get one of the rottweilers I was breeding."

"Have you been pretty close since then?"

"I'm as close to Rod as I am with anybody. He can live in this house until he's 50," Brent said, loud enough so Rod could hear. "He's like a son."

"So did you follow Rod's pro career closely?"

"Sure did. Even the Cincinnati years."

"I heard those were pretty bad."

Brent nodded.

"I once drove down to Cincinnati in my truck and went to training camp because I wanted to beat Bruce Coslet's ass." Brent seemed agitated at the mere thought.

"What happened?"

"Rod came out of practice and had to take me up to his room to calm me down."

Not only did I feel welcomed by the Ecklers, but I also got to know Rod better just by talking with Brent. His memories gave me perspective, as well as more background information for the story I planned to write about Rod.

Eventually, I completed the epic tale. It ran on the cover of the sports section on August 3, 2001, with a big picture of Rod sitting in a wooden chair on the front porch of the Ecklers' house. At the top of the story—next to the headline: PAYNE'S FULFILLED—is a smaller, close-up shot of Rod's hand, his Super Bowl ring featured prominently.

I was proud of the story, even though it wasn't hailed as much as my profile on Anders Nieters, the young cyclist who had leukemia— "Romie, you spin a fine ball of yarn," one editor told me about that one. Still, Rod's story garnered plenty of attention around the newsroom.

My coworkers were left scratching their heads as to how I had landed the scoop—the famous Rod Payne back in town. *Was it assigned to him? Did somebody at the football building tell him?* They were confounded even more when one of my bosses, the assistant sports editor who allowed me to write Rod's story, praised me for it in front of everyone.

"It reads good," he said. "So good it's like you didn't even write it."

"Very funny," I said as I logged on to my computer. I cracked a smile, knowing my coworkers had heard our exchange.

In the newsroom, jealousy is always present. This makes even the tiniest hint of favoritism for a reporter (especially one as low on the totem pole as I was), a topic for major gossip. But I wanted no part of this newsroom soap opera, so I decided to work on location for a few days. I grabbed my laptop and fled to one of the campus coffee shops.

I usually settled at the Starbucks near the State Theatre, where the *Blair Witch Project* had debuted the previous summer. A near-riot ensued when the theater couldn't accommodate the hundreds of extra students who wanted to get in. I was one of them, milling about the streets as the movie played, furious that I had just waited in line almost two hours for nothing.

Surrounded by a throng of summer-school students sipping cappuccinos and doing homework, I worked on stories for the paper, conducting an occasional interview by cell phone. I might call a coach at home, or an athlete I was writing about, then ask to speak to his or her parents, get their take on their son or daughter's athletic talents. I also dove into some of the ideas Rod and I had come up with for possible books. One night, I put together a string of pages for a children's book.

Sometimes I was interrupted from my typing by my cell phone. It was usually my boss, wondering where my next story was.

"It's coming," I said on one such occasion. "I'll e-mail it to you soon."

"But John told me you were working on it with him," my boss said, referring to the coworker I was paired with on our season-ending awards story, in which we honored the top high school athletes in the area. "Do you want to talk to him?"

"No, I talked to John earlier," I explained. "I told him I'd have my part in by eight."

I looked at my watch: 7:22.

"When have I ever let you down?" I asked.

After a pause, my boss replied, "Good luck, we're all counting on you." My boss said that all the time. I used to think he really meant it, but I had recently found out it was just a line from *Airplane*, one of his favorite movies.

Later, the phone rang again. I looked at my watch: 7:53. I decided if it was my boss, I was really going to give it to him.

A couple weeks before this, while having sushi with a girl I met during a night out with Rod and friends, he called me looking for a story I still had four hours to turn in. I really did give it to him then: "I told you this afternoon I'd have it in. So unless you hear otherwise, don't call me again!" I did this partly because I was upset he interrupted my date, but also to put on a show for the girl.

"Wow, you really talk to your boss like that?" she asked.

"Yup," I said as I dipped my yellowtail into a cup of soy sauce.

After the phone rang this time, I looked at the caller ID. It wasn't my boss—it was Rod.

"What's up, bro?" Rod asked.

"Just chillin' at the coffee shop, doing some writing."

"Same place?"

"Yep."

"I'll come by and scoop you up."

As I started to shut down my laptop, I remembered I had forgotten to e-mail my story to work. My boss would never have let me live that down. I opened my Internet connection, brought up the story, and sent it off. While I packed up my things, I was already envisioning Rod's truck—his bronze Suburban—pulling up to the curb across the street in a no parking zone I'd dubbed "MVP parking."

I looked around the coffee shop, where students were spending their prime nighttime hours studying calculus or accounting or some other nerve-racking undergraduate subject, and wondered how it could be that Rod was my friend. "Why am I taking calls from someone as recognizable in this town as an A-list celebrity?" I wondered.

As I exited the coffee shop, I was instantly swept away by the warm summer night. Michigan's campus was always fleet and alive that time of year, the cherished summer months when everything isn't as hectic. It was like a scene out of an old movie: the lampposts dotting the narrow roads; the glowing lights emanating from the marquee atop the State Theatre; the students exiting the corner ice cream shop with a double scoop in one hand and a backpack in the other (or a girl, if they were lucky). It was all a moment captured in time.

After I crossed the street and climbed into Rod's high-riding Suburban, I was greeted by my chauffeur's familiar refrain: "What's up, bro?"

Rod punched the truck into drive, and I was overcome by the intoxicating environment of the cab. The air was always so cool, despite the humidity outside, the cabin always dark, like the tables around the bar area of a fancy restaurant. The dashboard instruments emitted an entrancing glow. And the height of the truck—the elevated view of the road it gave us, all those cars down below— made me feel tall, confident . . . special.

It felt like it did when Dad sat me atop giant John Deere tractors at the Minnesota State Fair. I could see forever from the driver's seat of those green-and-yellow monsters, with Dad below, waving to me as the other fairgoers looked on.

It felt the same way in Rod's truck, like I could see the whole world in front of me and everyone was looking up at me.

⊷⊶ ≖✦≖ ⊷⊶

Those early days with Rod were a time in my life—similar to the years I spent trying to become a rock star on the streets of Hollywood (my efforts, I suppose, to regain that view from the top)—I can call, in a word, carefree. Although I was still weighed down by many problems, they never felt as heavy from inside the spacious cab of Rod's truck. In Rod's office, as he calls it—a massive "think tank" on wheels—I finally had the peace of mind I missed out on during the tumultuous years of my youth.

Much of that turmoil I don't hesitate to blame on my childhood friends, none of whom ever treated me like a true friend should. They never showed any interest in me, or asked for my opinion on things, or stuck up for me. Looking back, it's like I was their token friend, someone they let hang around just to make their circle of friends appear bigger. They never really let me in, like I had always hoped.

"Yeah, but look at me now," I thought as Rod turned the corner onto South State Street, my street. During the approach to my apartment, I wondered whether my childhood friends were doing anything with their lives now, aside from working at the same grocery stores they did in high school. During a recent trip home, I learned one of them had been promoted to the meat locker. Another had left the grocery-bagging business and had gotten a courier job. He lived in his mother's garage.

Even though I'd known Rod just a short time, he was already unlike any friend I'd ever had. Maybe this was why I sometimes had doubts our friendship would last. It just seemed too good to be true. These doubts, I'm certain, had a lot to do with my unfortunate past, which always seemed to hang around with me, corral me. I had to make a conscious effort to quell them, even in the sanctuary of Rod's truck—which, by the way, wasn't the only vehicle to have a nickname. My car, an Eclipse, was affectionately known as "the pod."

The times Rod and I needed agility over brute strength to get around town, or even to Detroit and back in a hurry, we jettisoned from my apartment in the slicker, more inconspicuous pod. Its compact size gave us a different, more common perspective on the journey: we were in the fray as opposed to towering above it.

The journeys to Motown were rare, but nonetheless unforgettable. Whether we passed through neighborhoods that time seemed to have left behind (boarded-up houses, fire-gutted buildings) or the lights and glamour of renovated downtown (Comerica Park, home of the Detroit Tigers; and the FOX Theatre, where I took my sushi date to see a stage rendition of *Grease*) Rod maneuvered the handier

Eclipse as gracefully as he did his leviathan of a truck, even under duress.

During one visit to Detroit, we got ambushed by a storm. We were already running late after trying on some suits at a clothing store owned by a friend of Rod's (his store, apparently, was only accessible by passing through those run-down neighborhoods), and I had to be at work in half an hour, six o'clock.

"It doesn't look good," I told Rod, knowing we were about 40 minutes from home.

"Don't worry, bro," Rod said, cranking up the windshield wipers. "I'll get you there."

We had just stopped at a drive-through and loaded up on burgers and fries. As Rod approached the freeway on-ramp, he latched his knees around the steering wheel and ripped the foil wrapper off his double bacon burger as rain pounded the windshield.

"Hand me my fries," Rod instructed me as he flew down the approach.

While the windshield wipers struggled to do their job, I glanced at the speedometer: 55 . . . 60 . . . 75 . . . 80 . . .

Detroit freeways are not for the timid. I became aware of this after I moved there from LA, where I developed my driving skills on the more laid-back interstates back home. (They're laid-back because there's so much traffic you don't move.) In D-Town, you either keep with the flow or get out of the way.

Once settled into a lane, Rod scooped a glob of tomatoes and pickles doused with ketchup and mayonnaise from his burger. He lowered his window to allow in a sideways-falling rain and, with a flick of his wrist, hurled the burger slush into the lane next to us, hoping not to hit the red Miata a couple car-lengths behind. During all of this, Rod seemed unfazed by the rain drenching the pod's dark-gray interior.

"You're getting wet," I told him, pointing out the obvious.

"It's mind over matter, bro—" Rod took a gargantuan bite of his burger—"if you don't mind, it don't matter."

Rod finally closed the window and began scanning the channels of the radio in search of a hip-hop station.

"You want me to get this?" I said, reaching for the dial.

"I got it," Rod mumbled, crowding me out with his tree trunk arm.

At the first note of his ring tone, Rod grabbed his cell phone and tucked it under his ear in a sleight-of-hand motion. Then he talked on the phone and ate his burger as calmly as if we were sitting in a corner booth at Wendy's, where we bought the food. I was too entertained by the sight—and at the same time shocked—to even think about eating my grilled chicken and bacon sandwich. If I had been driving in that hurricane, my heart would have been planted in my throat and my hands locked on 10 and 2. The food would have definitely had to wait.

"Here, take this," Rod said, handing me his crumpled-up wrapper.

"You must have finished this burger in three bites," I said.

Rod didn't respond; he was still on his phone call.

By the time I got to my sandwich, it was cold. But it still tasted pretty good.

In the end, we survived the journey—so did the driver of the Miata, even with mayonnaise and ketchup all over his windshield (at least we hoped he did). I also made it to work on time. Well, I was actually 15 minutes late, but thankfully, there are no time clocks in the journalism business. I wouldn't have been in it if there were.

The more adventures Rod and I took around town, the more people expected to see us together. Many of them asked him about me when I wasn't around—Rod's friends; former teammates; and business partners, such as those at the car-customizing shop he co-owned in Ann Arbor. Those guys were real cool with me, even though I was the new guy on the team, so to speak.

Conversely, some of Rod's acquaintances didn't condone our friendship. One I know for sure was a former classmate of Rod's, a lawyer who was just starting her career. At my apartment one afternoon, Rod started laughing when she came up in conversation. We were deciding what to do for dinner, and I suggested going to her place. We'd been there a couple of times, and it was usually pretty fun. The last time we went, we cooked pasta with sausages and peppers while listening to James Taylor, then watched a movie.

"What's so funny?" I asked Rod when he started chuckling about the lawyer.

"Oh, man. Did I tell you what she said?"

"No."

"She was giving me crap because I keep bringing you around."

"What did I do?"

"Nothing. She just doesn't understand why I'd want to hang around with a reporter. She's like, 'What does *he* bring to the party?'"

Sensing my shock, Rod added, "Don't worry, bro. She's just a frustrated woman. She's always been like that."

Still sensing my shock, he said, "She doesn't know how much you can learn by spending time with those different than you normally would. People like her live real sheltered lives."

Despite Rod's attempts to calm me, I was still surprised she had said that, and a little hurt.

"She never acted that way when I was with her," I said.

"Hey, brother, better to cut the grass and reveal the snakes than have 'em sneak up and bite you."

Although that didn't help much, I was at least comforted by Rod's reaction to the girl. If the first thing he does when a saboteur comes around is actually tell me about it, I knew there was no way he was ever going to be swayed by one.

The more Rod and I got to know each other, the more comfortable I felt telling him things. Eventually, I started to open up about my childhood friends.

"I was the only Jewish kid in the group," I told him. "Most of my neighborhood friends were Catholic or had no religion at all. But they knew every anti-Semitic slur in the book, and they weren't afraid to sling them at me whenever they wanted."

"That's terrible," Rod said. "You didn't need that. No one does."

I didn't tell Rod, but I regret having never done anything to stop them. For instance, the time they flicked matches at me on my way home from school, I just kept walking, never turning around to confront them.

Mom, for her part, never did anything to help me, because I never told her what was going on. How could I? How do you tell your mom something like that? Plus, she got home from work late, tired. She wanted to relax and forget about her day's troubles. It was just better to keep my problem inside, I figured. It was mine to deal with, anyway, not hers.

Religion, alas, wasn't the only thing that kept my peers and me on opposite sides of the pew.

"Most of the kids in my neighborhood had siblings, older and younger brothers or sisters," I told Rod. "So I was the 'spoiled' only child of the group. They also called me greedy, Jew Boy, a miser. Those were all words they used."

"And I was the only overweight one of the bunch," I added. "Fat, terrible at sports, unattractive to girls. I was also the only one who disappeared each summer and occasional winter to visit my dad. That's when I gained all my weight."

"What happened?"

"During one winter with him, when I was eight, I broke my leg skiing—on the bunny slope. With nothing to do over the following two months that I was kept out of school, I ate and watched television. It's no wonder I was chubby until high school. I probably still would be if Mom hadn't taken me to her personal trainer back then, Sam Scarber—Coach Sam, I called him. He's a former San Diego Charger and an actor—he was in that movie *Over the Top*, the arm-wrestling flick with Sylvester Stallone. He turned me into a thin man again."

"So what was the big deal about visiting your dad? Why would your friends care about that?"

"I didn't think it was a big deal until one of them actually told me they resented me for taking off each summer to Minnesota."

"Really?"

"I suppose they thought I was too good for them." Summer, it seems, is when most of the bonding times of youth are formed, far beyond the pastel walls of elementary school bungalows. "I can actually understand that," I told Rod. "I just don't think banishment—or being the court jester of the group—is a fair punishment for the crime."

"Hey, man. Those cats are out of your life now," Rod said. "We've all had idiots like that in our lives. I did. I was 'different' because of my size. Hey, you've already moved on. So let it go."

<hr>

Although Rod and I didn't talk about it as often as we did our other similarities, another common bond we shared was our fatherless upbringing. Whereas Rod made up for his lack of paternal guidance with help from his coaches, I had to rely on pure luck to get through my many trials of youth.

It's nice to think Dad's presence would have been helpful in getting me past those challenges (especially the teasing I got from my classmates, and the times they snatched the baseball cap I covered my bald head with and ran off into the playground with it), but I'm not sure I would have told him much about my plight, either. I think he would have really had to pry to get the information out of me. And judging by his actions on the whole over the years, I don't think he would have been up for the challenge.

Dad was great early on; he fought in court for visitation rights when I was a baby, then spoiled me with all the toys, Happy Meals, and trips to Dairy Queen I wanted during the summers. But in later years, he always avoided problems with me simply by turning his back on them—and sometimes me.

I told Rod a story that illustrated this.

"It was summer 1985, the summer of my Bar Mitzvah. I was acting up, mimicking Dad and that sort of thing. So Dad woke me up one morning, drove me to the airport, and put me on a plane back to Los Angeles—with two months remaining on my visit. And he did it without calling my mom to tell her I was coming home."

"That's pretty harsh."

"Yeah. I'll never forget the look on Dad's face as I walked down the jetway that day. 'Bye, Stevie,' he said as he waved good-bye, then backpedaled into the terminal and around the corner out of view. Mom had to find another place for me to stay in Minnesota, near Beth El Synagogue in Minneapolis, so I could keep studying with my Hebrew teacher there. The ceremony was a few weeks away. Mom did find a family to take me in: the mother of the family was a childhood friend of hers."

"What happened to your dad?"

"I was told the rabbi at Beth El banned him from the synagogue when he called the morning of my Bar Mitzvah, asking to participate. I haven't had any contact with him since he sent me home."

"That's abandonment," Rod said.

"Yeah, but I remembered being sort of a pain in the ass around that time. Maybe I deserved the heave-ho."

"You were just 13. You didn't know any better. Plus, you were never raised with any discipline."

Rod was right. Coming home to an empty apartment every day, then watching TV until late in the evening, when Mom finally arrived home with a bag of fast food, afforded me many liberties while growing up—yet very little else, I'm afraid.

⚬ ⚬≒⚬ ⚬

There were a lot of things that drove me to Michigan: a higher education, a sense of community, and clean air to breathe after a lifetime of ingesting smog and traffic fumes in LA. But the more I got to know Rod, the more I realized the biggest reason I left home was to build up my long-term sense of self-worth. To make up for never having those fatherly lessons, or a true friend, someone I could always count on—whether I was fat or Jewish or a pain in the butt.

CHAPTER NINE

I Put Bricks in That Building!

⊷ ≡◈≡ ⊷

"Each time a man stands up for an ideal . . . or strikes out
against injustice, he sends forth a tiny ripple of hope."
—ROBERT F. KENNEDY

A loud, penetrating noise wakes me from a deep sleep. It's coming from the IV machine, an incessant beeping. It won't stop. It's driving me crazy.

The bag in the machine is empty, which is causing the racket. Still, it will take forever for a nurse to come in here and change it, even if I keep the call button pressed.

Where is everyone? Rod's not in his cot; Mom is gone too. So I have to deal with this on my own. And this isn't some alarm clock I can just turn off—a nurse has to do it.

Finally, one arrives. She offers no explanation for her delay as she changes the bag of clear liquid food, which stops the annoying beeping.

Because I can't eat solid food—or rather I won't; it hurts my chest too much—this IV is all that's keeping me from shrinking into a hospital robe on a hanger. I've lost 10 or 15 pounds so far, and I'm guessing that's only the beginning.

I look at the nurse, a heavyset lady with light-brown hair. I've never seen her before.

"Where is everyone?" I ask.

"Your mother and the big guy went to get something to eat."

The big guy? I force a smile, opting not to explain to this nurse the severity of her error, like I did to the Michigan State lady.

Rod, to be sure, is not just some "big guy" here to keep me company. By delivering his well-chosen, forceful words in person rather than over the phone, Rod has pulled me through the initial challenges of my disease—the blood transfusions, the mental struggles, the fear. His presence alone is a motivating force. As I told my mom, "You're here to hold my hand; Rod's here to kick me in the butt."

Besides that, Rod has helped me more than I can ever repay by eating the so-called food delivered to me three times a day. Because my immune system is so weak, doctors have me on a low-bacteria diet. Everything they bring me—chicken broth, sugarless Jell-O (always orange), and bland scrambled eggs in the morning—tastes as horrible as nonfat milk or diet cola when you're expecting regular. The aftertaste alone can kill you.

Since Rod has always been far less picky than I when it comes to what he eats, he has attacked my low-bacteria meals with gusto, like the two-inch-thick filet mignon and garlic mashed potatoes he had at training table following two-a-day practices at Michigan.

I'm sure Rod is feasting on something just as satisfying tonight. Meanwhile, I watch the nurse hang my dinner from the pole.

Not being able to eat is bad enough. But the worst part isn't even the pain. I don't have any taste buds. The chemo has wreaked havoc with my mouth, and it doesn't help that Pizza Hut and McDonald's have so many commercials on TV. You just don't notice things like this until you're not able to eat anymore.

The medicines, for their part, are causing my skin to crawl. I feel like I've been digging ditches all day in the hot sun. And I'm not able to just jump in the shower like I normally would. I'm tied up with so many tubes it's a major production getting me out of this bed. I'm allowed one shower a day, and it's an exhausting affair—even with the plastic bench in the shower to sit on. Afterward, I collapse facedown into my bed, staying there a good 20 minutes before I have the energy just to roll over.

When I finally do, I become determined to find a comfortable position. When—or if—I can, it lasts only a few minutes: parts of my legs, butt, and back have already begun to atrophy, causing them to alternate between tingling and numbness.

I get up only to throw up or to pull more gobs of hair out of my head, which has steadily been falling out since I arrived. This reminds me of my first cancer, when clumps of my hair inexplicably surfaced in the swimming pool when Mom and I visited Nana in Palm Springs. Luckily her neighbors' grandchildren and I were playing Marco Polo, so they either had their eyes closed or were searching for a hiding place while I paddled around scooping up my hair.

Today, I couldn't care less how my hair looks anyway—it was already thinning before I got sick. I'm more concerned about the pain in my chest, which is so intense I hold my morphine pump like a gun to my hip, triggering it every two minutes. I've been using this pump since I arrived, when my throat started to burn whenever I tried to eat.

The burning was so severe that Mom and her brother, Larry, who's visiting me from Minneapolis with his wife, Judy, vigorously rubbed my chest and upper back as I swallowed. The morphine gave me only minimal relief, as if I was already becoming immune to its effects. Despite Mom and Uncle Larry's noble efforts, it still felt like a hot coal had been dropped down my throat, a pain so harsh I actually started to cry.

That was the last of my eating.

As I continue to swallow these thoughts, the phone rings. The ring is twice as loud as the beeping was, so I scramble to answer it.

It's Rod on his cell phone.

"Where are you?" I ask calmly even though that ring jolted me like a scene out of a scary movie.

"We just ate at this place called Jerry's Deli. We're going to your mom's apartment now to pick up some things."

"Cool," I say. "Take your time."

Rod sounds relaxed during his first trip away from the hospital. Before he hangs up, he regales me with the menu he enjoyed at Jerry's: New York steak, Caesar salad, triple-layer chocolate cake. Rod has no idea what he's doing to me, but I'm not mad at him. I'm happy he's getting a reprieve from this horrible place. I wish I had one.

After I hang up the phone, I try to drift back asleep. Before I can, it hits me: Rod is going to my mom's apartment, the one I grew up in.

⊷ ⇌⬩☰⬩ ⊶

I first arrived at 10883 Palms Boulevard, no more than a 15-minute drive from the hospital, when I was three years old.

After crawling up the stairs to Apartment 6 on the left side of the second floor, I stumbled into a large bedroom full of toys. There were so many I could barely walk on the green shag carpet. The brown rocking horse (with springs for bounce), which sat by the window in the back of the room, still jumps out in my memory. All of the toys do, including the same pop-pop machine Rod once whacked his refrigerator with to get to Mrs. Payne's chocolate cake.

Although none of those toys remained in the apartment past a few years, the clutter I found that first day in my bedroom never went away. Never was my bedroom without wall-to-wall posters—of cartoons as a kid, then of sports as I got older. Next came music posters (Mötley Crüe, Ozzy), girls (Farrah, Heather Thomas), and sports again (namely the Miami Dolphins, my favorite football team growing up because I idolized Dan Marino). No matter what transformations I went through over the years, my bedroom always reflected them.

Decorating my bedroom was a labor of love to me, a reflection of my creative side. Yet, despite my regular attempts at upkeep over the years, I often felt uncomfortable having people see it. The walls alone, chipped and discolored—and littered with endless tiny pieces of Scotch tape—were an embarrassment. That went for the apartment in general, which wasn't much tidier. (Mom, after working all day at the doctor's office, had very little time or energy to clean when she got home.)

Still, even though Rod is on his way to see that mess in my bedroom—the trinkets, photos, and sports and music paraphernalia stashed in every nook—I don't mind. I know I don't have to hide anything from Rod. I've tried that before—hiding things from Rod—and all it did was nearly cost me our friendship.

— ≍✦≍ —

It was supposed to be a special day: Rod wanted to take me to Schembechler Hall to show me where he built his reputation as a warrior in college. Within those hallowed walls, Rod routinely took over weightlifting competitions, bench-pressing more than anyone else on the team. It's where he learned all those valuable lessons of manhood and where he's now respected more than ever; the current Michigan football players are mesmerized by his Super Bowl ring as much as I was the first time I saw it.

Rod worked out at the Building nearly every day before stopping by my apartment, usually in the late morning or early afternoon. One day he dropped by, same time as usual, only he didn't walk through the door.

"Get ready, bro," he said, taking an empty look around the apartment as if he was thinking about another place entirely.

"What do you mean?" I asked. I had just woken up. My mind was on cereal and TV, not jumping in the shower and going someplace.

"C'mon," he said, rubbing his chin. "Let's go over there."

"Where?"

"To the Building."

My heart dropped. I instantly recalled the rules of engagement over there: the Building was strictly off-limits to the media. Some reporters called it Fort Michigan.

Only on rare occasions were writers allowed inside the multimillion-dollar training facility, usually for an event the football team wanted the media to cover, such as the annual summer skills camp, a major recruiting tool because it attracted thousands of high school athletes from across the country. I covered the camp the year before I met Rod, and had an eerie feeling about the whole experience—like I simply didn't belong there.

Although reporters need no background checks or retina exams to enter Schembechler Hall—only a written preapproval—it's still unsettling for them to walk through the building with their press passes dangling. (Imagine walking through a lion's den holding 30 pounds of raw meat.) I felt like a visitor walking through a prison, the inmates' eyes studying me the whole time I was there. But that's not why I didn't want to go with Rod on the tour.

A few months after writing my summer camp story, I penetrated the walls of Schembechler Hall when I wasn't preapproved to be there. And all hell broke loose.

— ⊷ ⧫ ⊶ —

It started when I showed up at work one weekday afternoon around lunchtime. As I began to write a story, the editor assigned to the sports desk that day received a call. He was told that Drew Henson, Michigan football's starting quarterback—and the most hailed newcomer to the team, the golden boy from nearby Brighton tabbed to replace Tom Brady, who left to the NFL a few months earlier—had been injured during a recent practice. The season was only a week away, so that was big news. And since the *Ann Arbor News* is the newspaper of record for the Michigan football team, we *had* to get the story.

My editor hung up with the informant and turned to me. I looked around. I was the only reporter in the sports department.

"Go over to there and find out what you can, Rom."

I knew he meant Schembechler Hall. I also knew he was aware of the rule about the media. But he offered no specifics on how to get into the place. He had confidence in me, however, and that was all that mattered.

I got in my Eclipse and drove at light speed through downtown Ann Arbor, snaking cars the whole way to Schembechler Hall. I was determined to get the story—no matter what it took. This was the big one.

Last time I'd landed the big one—the Charles Woodson story—I was marched into the glass-enclosed office of the executive editor. He gave me a pat on the back and a "way to nudge Woodson into talking to you." He knew no other media source could, including both Detroit papers as well as the local NBC affiliate, which were live on the scene. The next day, after the story appeared in every major newspaper in the country—I'M ONLY A HUMAN BEING, in the *New York Post*, was my favorite headline—I was promoted to my College Notes job.

Because I knew Schembechler Hall was out of bounds for reporters, I had to try something other than knocking on the front door and flashing my press pass. I stashed my car at the rear of the parking lot and went around back hoping to catch a glimpse of practice from back there. I got lucky—a janitor was throwing out the trash. As he emptied the cans into a receptacle a few feet away from me, I slipped through the door he left open.

At this point, my entire being was consumed with getting the story. As I entered the main corridor of the building, I was so lost in thought I ran up to the first player I found. I accosted David Terrell, the star receiver and future first-round draftee of the Chicago Bears. I stood in front of him, my tape recorder in my sweaty palm, showering him with questions about Henson.

"What's the extent of the injury? Did you see it happen? Is there an update? Will Henson be able to play?"

Terrell didn't answer. He just stared at me as he marched toward the locker room with a pack of teammates behind him. They had just gotten off the field after practice and were still in uniform, helmets on, dripping with sweat. I backpedaled, staying one step ahead of Terrell. I was waiting for just one answer, one sound bite—anything. Just then, an assistant coach flanking the players spotted me.

"Hey! How'd you get in here? Get the hell out of here!"

He shouted so loudly, the entire team stopped and looked at me— the *entire* Michigan football team. I was breathless. I felt like a police informant whose wire had just fallen out in a room full of Mafia members. I was dead.

I began to search for an exit, slowly at first, then faster as I felt the tension build. All of a sudden, in a rash move inspired by a combination of fear and the need to still get the story, I made a break for the stairs leading up to the coaches' office. (I remembered the stairs from the time I interviewed Jim Herrmann, Michigan's defensive coordinator, in his office for the summer camp story. He was the director of the event, overseeing more than 1,500 kids.) Bad move—I trapped myself upstairs. In seconds, a team spokesman tracked me down. He summarily escorted me downstairs and out the front door. I was surprised he didn't throw me onto the concrete. *And don't come back, ya bum!*

When Rod offered to take me on a tour of the Building, I recalled the Henson incident and quickly tried to get out of it. I reminded him of the rule about the media, but he just laughed it off.

"I'll tell them you're with me," he said, already heading out the door. "C'mon, let's go."

I had no chance. If I continued to resist, he'd want to know the real reason I didn't want to go. I certainly didn't want to offer that information. Besides, school hadn't started yet, so there was probably light traffic in the Building. I figured we probably wouldn't run into any problems. Plus, I wanted to get a tour of the place my friend holds so dear.

Things started off well. Rod and I walked past the secretary in the lobby without incident. She didn't even give us a second look, hardly lifting her head out of a magazine. Rod and I then passed through a pair of large blue doors, which placed us at the beginning of a long corridor that split the Building in two.

Straight ahead, about 30 yards from where we stood, I saw the glass doors leading out to the practice fields. This was where the players came in from practice when I rushed them during the Henson debacle. Above the doors, painted on a long, wooden beam, it read, THOSE WHO STAY WILL BE CHAMPIONS.

Rod began the tour by pointing out the pictures and plaques of some of the former Michigan football greats.

"Here's mine," Rod said.

It was next to Woodson's picture and 1997 MVP plaque, a framed picture of Rod on the field during a game. Below it, engraved on a small, gold nameplate, were some of Rod's accolades: "First-team All-American; two-time First-team All–Big Ten; 1996 co-captain and most valuable player." (And, according to a press release I had seen in the office recently, one of Michigan's "Offensive Linemen of the Century.") Next to the nameplate was Rod's 1996 MVP plaque. It was a bronze piece that jumped off the wall.

Seeing the plaque right in front of me helped me finally match the myth with the man, this legend that is my friend. It reminded me of a bust in the NFL Hall of Fame, a fascinating sight. I was glad I had decided to go on the tour.

Next stop was the equipment room, a few paces up the corridor and to the right. I remembered seeing it during my first visit to Schembechler Hall. I had been interviewing Herrmann when we passed by it. Even in that fleeting glance, a world of amazing things caught my eye.

For a moment, it reminded me of the first equipment room I ever saw, in junior high school. I'll never forget those lockers full of basketballs, volleyballs, kickballs, even jump ropes. Now, during this close-up look at the Michigan football team's equipment room, the first thing I noticed was all the bright colors inside it. They were painted all over the Big Ten football helmets that sat atop wide, blue lockers surrounding the room. The lockers stretched nearly to the ceiling and towered over a large, metal worktable in the middle of the room.

"Those are the teams we've pounded over the years," Rod said about the helmets, his pride as palpable as the gouges covering every inch of them.

After paying my respects to the fallen Big Ten teams of the past—Minnesota, Illinois, and Northwestern among them—Rod led me into a narrow hallway in the rear of the room. Around the bend I saw more lockers.

They lined both sides and also stretched to the ceiling. Stored inside was everything the team needed to take the field: helmets, footballs, uniforms, and pads of all kinds. It was a sports memorabilia fan's fantasyland. And it had a distinct smell: a combination of sweat and leather that only an athlete could love. It made me wish I had done something more after I saw that equipment room in junior high, like maybe checked out some of the equipment after school, instead of running home to a TV and a La-Z-Boy, then waiting for Mom to come home with that bag of fast food.

"Cool, ain't it?" Rod asked, beaming me back to the moment.

"Yeah," I said, marveling at all those pristine jerseys. I imagined how much they would cost in the student store—a fortune.

As we walked out of the room, Rod told me that Michigan's equipment room was better than most NFL rooms he'd seen over the years. And he said that Jon Falk, Michigan's longtime equipment manager, was by far *the* coolest equipment manager he'd ever known.

Rod shared with me what Falk says whenever a reporter asks him what's the sweetest Big Ten championship he's won in his 20-plus years in Ann Arbor?

"The next one," Rod said, mimicking Falk, holding up an empty finger where the new ring presumably would go.

Rod and I strolled through the corridor, taking in the sights and enjoying the powerful air conditioning. (Compared to the outside, it was like a meat locker in there.) We were headed for the locker room on the left side of the building, just before the glass doors.

There were actually two locker rooms, Rod pointed out—one for the juniors and seniors, the other for the underclassmen.

As I stepped into the plush, upperclassmen locker room, its all-blue decor immediately sucked me in—the carpet, lockers, chairs, and walls were all painted in an entrancing deep blue. Next, I noticed the players' names and uniform numbers above each locker on engraved plates, as if they were CEOs of Fortune 500 companies. This was a big leap from the humble underclassmen locker room, which wasn't much nicer than a high school room—and smelled even worse. The juniors and seniors' room, meanwhile, smelled appropriately fresh and stately, like fine cologne.

I was feeling sort of regal myself as Rod and I continued on the tour. I knew it was because of my tour guide, who made me feel like I belonged there in some small way just because I was with him.

"Let's go check out the weight room," Rod said.

As we cut across the corridor, I recalled the story Rod told me about the freshman from Ypsilanti, the one who pulled that rope for 20 minutes, falling all over himself as his teammates stood by yelling "This is how we do things at Michigan!" I couldn't wait to see the weight room.

As that thought filled my mind, it was immediately eclipsed by the sight of the football team's portly sports information director walking out of an office adjacent to the weight room. SIDs serve as the liaison between the team and the media. Every team has one, and I knew this one recognized me, if only from my picture in the paper. Since he was also the eyes and ears of the building, I was sure he knew all about the Henson incident as well, even though I didn't remember having seen him that day.

"What's up?" Rod said to the fellow, having no clue of the trouble that might be afoot.

There was no answer, just a glare from the SID.

"You shouldn't be here," he said, looking right at me.

I knew this had all been a bad idea.

Rod appeared confused. This was a first for him, always being in control as he was. This frightened me even more. I'm certain Rod never imagined he would actually have to say something to someone about me being in the building. I mean, clearly, I was with *him*.

"Chill out, man," Rod said to the fellow, sensing the tension in the air. "I know media ain't allowed in here, but he's with me. I'm just showing him around."

I hoped that would do it.

"The coaches aren't going to like that," the SID said.

I noticed the SID was practically trembling, as if he thought *he* was actually going to get in trouble for my being there—like he was an accessory to a crime.

"What do you mean coaches aren't going to like that?" Rod asked.

"Ask him," the SID said, motioning at me.

After an awkward pause, Rod and I did an about-face and walked in the direction of the glass doors. I could feel the SID's eyes burning a hole in my back until we were outside and around the corner. Under the intense sun, I felt more nervous.

I didn't want to come clean; I was too afraid of the consequences. My invitation inside the world of a professional athlete might be revoked. Or worse, my friendship with Rod, over.

I thought I might say the SID had me confused with somebody else, or that I didn't know what he was talking about. I immediately chose otherwise—deciding it better to get things out in the open, like a suspect coming clean to investigators because it might lessen his sentence. Cooperation, I knew, was my only ally.

I told Rod about the Henson fiasco, intentionally leaving out the parts about sneaking through the back door and being thrown out. I decided there was no way I could tell him that, not under the spotlight of that merciless sun.

As we paced the end-zone lines of the practice fields, Rod didn't say a word. With his hand to his chin, he looked like a judge listening to the testimony of a key witness.

At one point, while I fumbled through the details of my case, I took a quick look around. We were actually pacing the Michigan football team's practice fields, those so guarded as to be sacred. I realized this was where many of the stories Rod told me during our interviews took place. I also knew I clearly didn't belong there. This encounter we'd had with the SID assured me of that.

When we arrived at my apartment a short time later, Rod stopped his truck in the driveway. He put it in park, took a deep breath, and tactfully started to admonish me.

"Michigan football is a family," he said. "So when you did what you did, you disrespected the whole family." Rod's disappointment filled the cab, making me feel much smaller than I usually did in there.

"There are reasons for those rules," Rod continued. "So much stuff happens behind those doors—so much that has to do with the building of a team. Whether you like it or not, it's not your place to be in there. How would you like it if someone busted into your house, with your family there, and wrote all kinds of stuff about how you handle things inside your home. You'd want blood."

I sat silently, thinking maybe I should say something about how Michigan football is a public institution, and everybody wants to know about it—that it's my job to supply them with that information. But that would only lump me even further into the group of journalists that Rod so dislikes. So I just listened carefully, trying to understand what he was saying. It was a humbling situation. The most humbling I'd ever been in.

Eventually, it sunk in—how wrong I was. I felt as though I had fallen too far from Rod's graces to ever make my way back.

Rod stopped his lecture, but a moment later, he picked it up again.

"Michigan made me the man I am today," he said, staring into the midday glare on the windshield, "but it doesn't own me. I can bring anybody I want in there."

He was not done.

"Coaches wouldn't *like it* if you were there?" he asked, still glaring at the windshield. "Forget that! That's *my* MVP plaque on the wall!

"I put bricks in that building!"

Silence followed, giving me a chance to think.

I'd always known Rod stood for more than just football. But now I knew he stood for character and upholding the values his mom taught him, just as much as those his coaches did. He was a team player without the proverbial team politics. It was refreshing, even though the way I came to discover this still hurt.

Rod repeated to me how wrong I was. The next time an editor sends me out on a kamikaze mission, he said, I should think about what's more important: my career or my character.

"He doesn't care what happens to you," Rod said. "He just wants his story. Don't be like them, all those punks in your profession. Stand up for what you know, because I just told you what it's like. You don't have any more excuses."

Finally, Rod concluded his lecture.

"Yeah, that wasn't cool what you did," he said, his tone reverting to its normal decibel level. "But you were with *me*."

—⊷ ≖✦≖ ⊶—

As I climbed down from the cab, I thought about how I'd already learned more from Rod about being a man and standing up for a belief than anyone had ever even tried to teach me before. For that, I would always be grateful, no matter what happened between us.

Still, as I watched Rod drive off, I hoped that wouldn't be the last time I ever saw him again or climbed into that cab.

CHAPTER TEN

Catch Me If You Can

❮❮✦❯❯

"Nobody can make you feel inferior without your consent."
—ELEANOR ROOSEVELT

My concern over never seeing Rod again after our trip to Schembechler Hall was short-lived. He showed up at my apartment the next day. And while that only mildly surprised me (considering the lambasting he gave his former coaches), what stunned me was what happened next: nothing.

Rod said hello at the door, then headed to the kitchen to rustle up a can of chowder. As he poured the soup into a bowl and stuck it in the microwave, I wondered when he was going to bring up our confrontation with the SID.

I was sure he wanted a better explanation for what sent that fellow into such a tizzy. I felt he had to wonder about the embarrassing incident at the Building, now that he'd had a chance to sleep on it. Apparently, he didn't. In fact, he never said another word about the incident—not that day, not ever.

I found this to be one of Rod's pet peeves: harboring grievances only to bring them up at a later date. It's almost against his religion to do that, a sign of cowardice. Deal with things now, when they matter.

This is something I've always tried to do since I met Rod, one of the many things.

⊷ ⊨⊧ ⊶

Could it be any harder getting my bed on wheels into the elevator? It bangs against the walls as an orderly tries to steer me into the shaft. When he finally does manage the feat, I roll past a straggly haired woman seated on a metal barstool near the controls. She looks angry. I'd be too, if I had to sit there all day holding the "open" button for patients like me. I continue to look at her, but she doesn't return the glance. She just hits the "B" button.

I've been down there before—to the basement for treatments—and don't want to go. It's like a graveyard down there in that labyrinth of hallways.

On my first trip to the basement, for a radiation treatment, I was greeted by broken-down X-ray machines, large laundry bins full of soiled linens, and all of those patients. They were in wheelchairs; gurneys; or, like me, beds, waiting outside treatment rooms. Most of them were alone, their emotional pain as clear as the unmistakable hospital smell filling the hallways.

That smell took me back 20 years.

Mom would pick me up from school early, and we'd make the short drive to the hospital—*this* hospital—where I'd have radiation and chemotherapy treatments, doctor consultations, and the occasional CAT scan (a three-dimensional X-ray). The chemo trips were followed by three or four days of incapacitating nausea. It was so intense I often had to sleep on the bathroom floor, using a folded-up bath towel as my pillow. That way I could be ready for when the nausea attacked me again.

Mom had discovered my illness—or at least realized there was a problem—when she gave me my nightly bath. She noticed my legs were covered in bruises. "What happened?" she asked with worry as I stepped into the tub. "I don't know," I said. "I keep falling for no reason."

I don't think I've ever completely recovered from those long nights on the bathroom floor, when I'd sit up every hour and spill everything inside of me down the toilet. Neither has Mom, I believe, as all she could do was sit quietly in the adjacent bedroom, praying her only child would soon get some peace. By the time Mom would come into the bathroom to check on me, I would already be passed out in the corner, where the head of the bathtub meets the wall.

I remember those painful nights now, while I prepare for my third trip to the basement. The only difference from my first two visits and now, as I continue to stare at the elevator operator, is that Rod will be with me.

⋅⋅ ▰◆▰ ⋅⋅

It's Rod's second day in LA. He's in the elevator, right beside me. He'll watch me have another lumbar puncture, which is also called a spinal tap. Unlike the movie about the fictional band, real-life spinal taps are no laughing matter and are much more serious than radiation. During the radiation zaps, I just lie on my back on a cold, hard table and listen to classical music as a laser (or whatever it is) penetrates my brain. During the spinal taps, a four-inch needle is inserted into the base of my spine, first to remove cancerous fluids, then to inject powerful chemotherapy.

Doctors have scheduled a dozen of these lumbar punctures, along with a dozen radiation treatments, to help get me into remission, or reduce the 80-percent diseased white blood cells circulating through my body to less than five percent. That's the goal, but it's going to be difficult to reach.

Before the lumbar puncture begins, they make me sign a waiver stating that if anything goes wrong (i.e., the doctor has an unsteady hand, hits a nerve, and paralyzes me), I will not sue the hospital. Not the most reassuring feeling as I scribble my John Hancock.

As the elevator door closes and we plummet to the frigid realm, I start to envision the procedure. I begin wiggling my fingers and toes, as if it's the last time I'll be able to pull off this simple task. I continue to watch the operator sit on the stool and stare at the controls. She seems oblivious to my plight, as if she's wearing blinders. "Just another patient going to the basement," she must be thinking.

She's in her own world. It's a place I'm starting to go right now. I know I won't be there long, however. Rod would never allow it.

Whenever I'd fall into one of my funks in Michigan—either worrying about my next story, thinking about my past, or just zoning out at the TV—there would always be that knock at the door. Rod.

"Go away," I'd think for the first second or two after the knock. "Let me dwell in my pity." But in the next moment, I'd pull myself off the couch and walk to the door, leaving my worries behind. Everything would be fine then—I would have beaten the demons or whatever had strangled my energy into submission that day.

Although I'm confident in Rod's ability to motivate me, I'm sure his inaugural trip to the basement will be just as startling as was mine. I warn him of this, but he tells me not to worry. I know he still has no idea what he's in for.

The farther the elevator car plunges, the more I feel the basement's chill. When it jars to a halt and the door finally opens, the cold and dampness pour in like a wall of icy seawater slicing through the *Titanic*'s hull.

As we enter the hallway, my anxiety turns to dizziness. I feel washed away in the ever-increasing panic. I become woozy as the elevator door closes behind me. It sounds like one of the watertight doors closing after the *Titanic* plunged into an iceberg in the freezing North Atlantic. I'm starting to feel like one of the lookouts in the crow's nest that night so long ago—like there's impending doom ahead, and I just can't see it.

Please be over soon!

The orderly pushing my bed is a young Hispanic fellow. Rod and I can't communicate with him. I notice it's taking much longer to get to my treatment than before. We've passed by the same landmarks—an elderly lady in a wheelchair, for one—about three times. "See," I say to Rod, who has been quietly in tow, "this is what I've had to deal with down here."

Finally, we stop. The orderly appears confused, scratches his head, and looks around. *What the heck is he doing?*

A moment later, we resume the journey. After taking another lap around the basement, passing corridor after corridor—this place *is* like a labyrinth—the orderly steers me to the side of the hallway. He stops the bed, sets the parking brake, and rushes off.

Rod and I look at each other in disbelief.

"Where is he going?" I ask. "For directions?"

This is absurd. Neither of us says a word. We just wait for the guy to return, to take me to the treatment room and end this craziness.

As the minutes go by, I yearn for my room upstairs, where it is much warmer than in these hallways. I continue to think about the *Titanic*, how cold the water must have felt that night. I think about my great-grandfather, Nana's Russian immigrant dad, Isadore Lavintman. Papa, as we called him, must have been a young man at the time of *Titanic's* sinking. I wish I had had a chance to talk to him about that era in world history before he died prior to my first cancer. Life and death seem to be so closely related these days, it makes me wish I'd done a lot of things before now.

A few more minutes go by—still no sign of the driver. I look at a clock on the wall: ten minutes have elapsed. Twelve minutes. Fifteen!

I start to feel sick. Rod, I can hear, is grumbling also. I'm not even looking at him. I'm just staring at the plasterboard panels in the ceiling, trying to sooth my nausea by playing mind games.

"You're OK," I tell myself. "You'll be back in your room soon. Soon this will all be over."

"I hope he gets back quickly," I say.

I'm trying to take the pain, be a trooper, hang in there. But it's hard.

"I don't feel so well," I say softly.

Rod is still grumbling. He can hear the urgency in my voice. I know it.

A few minutes later, I'm about to ask Rod to go find someone—a doctor, another patient, *anyone*—to help us find the treatment room.

"I feel like I'm going to throw up," I say.

Without warning, Rod grabs ahold of the bed and kicks off the parking break. I feel a heavy jerk.

"Enough of this," Rod says, as he merges us into the basement traffic, like he did that rainy day on I-94. "I'm taking you back upstairs."

"Hurry, I can't make it much longer."

"I got you, bro," Rod says, picking up speed. "Don't worry. We just have to find an elevator."

We soon discover for ourselves how hard it is to navigate these hallways. Corner after corner we turn, but no luck. As Nana would say: there are about as many elevators down here as there are pigs.

"Where's the damn elevator?" Rod gripes from behind me. "Every hallway looks the same."

After another lap around the basement, we approach a group of orderlies. They're standing outside a break room, talking and sipping coffee. I want to tell Rod to stop and ask them for directions. But as we get closer, I realize that's not a good idea: they don't appear friendly, worse than the elevator operator. One, to my surprise, shouts at us as we pass.

"Hey, you can't do that!" His cohorts stare in disbelief, their coffee cups frozen near their lips. "Only hospital personnel can transport patients!"

Rod turns around to see who's yelling, but does not stop.

In fact, he goes faster, as if to say, "Try and stop me." I imagine that'll be the end of it, our confrontation with the orderlies.

"Stop!" one of them yells.

I turn around. Two of them are chasing us.

Are they kidding? Chasing a 300-pound bed hijacker?

I prop myself up so I can see ahead of us to navigate. The bed is clumsy. We start bouncing off the walls: first softly, then harder as Rod begins flinging me around corners.

"Get out of the way," I motion with my hand to pedestrians. "Runaway bed."

I grab the guardrails of the bed. I always wondered why these things are here. I continue to navigate.

"Make a left here," I say to Rod. "I see the hallway we came through up ahead. The elevator might be there."

As we turn onto a straightaway, I lay my head back and watch how quickly the rectangular lights above us pass by. They're in between the plasterboard panels I was looking at earlier. They look like one long strand of light at this speed. I can see our reflection in them. It reminds me of a reel of film passing through a projector, frame by frame. It seems like Rod and I are starring in one of those old, silent movies, the slapstick variety that take place in a hospital and feature this exact type of tomfoolery.

I begin to smile. I crane my neck back, trying to get a look at Rod. He's smiling too. Soon, we're both laughing as we careen down the hallways.

I whip my head forward when the bed strikes something in our path. No harm done, just an empty table. We keep moving. So do the orderlies, still in hot pursuit.

Although I fear an accident is inevitable, I'm thrilled to realize I no longer feel sick or cold. I'm not wiggling my toes anymore either. And as we pass by those many patients outside the rooms, some of them smile at us, including that old lady we keep passing. I make eye contact with her; she smiles at me, and I can tell Rod and I have managed to take away some of her pain. For that reason alone, I believe all of this is worthwhile.

Soon the chase ends—mercifully and without harm done to Rod or me or any in our wake.

Gasping for air, one of the orderlies, a young fellow with a mound of black hair demands to know where we're going. We try to explain that his Spanish-speaking colleague abandoned us, but he doesn't follow.

"What room are you in?" he demands, still sucking wind.

"Ten twenty," I say, offering nothing else.

The orderly wisely chooses not to scold the enormous bedjacker. Instead, he ushers us to the closest elevator and back to our room.

It's a long, quiet ride up. Rod and I purse our lips, trying not to laugh. This is where we wanted to go all along. And now we get a police escort!

I glance at the officer—I mean "orderly." He's still breathing hard, trying to compose himself. It feels like Rod and I are in grade school, like we just got into trouble on the playground and are being escorted to the principal's office by a teacher. Who would have known this trip to the basement would be so much fun?

Safely back in our room, Rod and I thank the young man for his help (facetiously, of course) and wait to see what he says. He just leaves in a huff, giving us a frustrated swivel of the head instead of any words. Good choice.

Now alone, Rod and I wonder whether my doctors will hear about what's happened, that I missed my treatment.

"Will there be an investigation?" I ask Rod as he lies down on his cot, flipping on the television.

"I don't know, bro," he says, letting out a prolonged sigh. "I don't know." Rod, of course, doesn't care about the consequences. Especially not when it comes to helping out a friend. I know there's nothing more important to him than that.

Rod's mom was the first to make this point clear to me. Before I got sick, I had a few chances to talk to her about Rod. Our conversations usually explained a lot about this former professional football player who was becoming my friend.

"He used to get into fistfights a lot," Mrs. Payne once told me. "Teachers thought Rod was a problem, but they didn't know the whole story."

"The whole story?"

"Rod would just help out anybody in trouble if they needed it. Rod was always for the underdog."

That statement floated in the air for so long, I was able to see it, feel it. It made me wonder whether Rod knew I was an underdog as well.

"That's just Rod," his mom added, as if she was reading my mind, "standing up for those who can't do it for themselves."

When Rod dropped by my apartment later that day, I told him what his mom had said, that he's always been for the underdog. He seemed to go into an instant state of reflection.

"Yeah," he said, "because I knew how they felt. I was picked on as a kid, too, for being chubby. But then it stopped."

"How'd it stop?" I waited for Rod's answer from the kitchen table. He was sitting on the couch, watching television. He shot me a look that told me to listen up.

"Because I fought back."

As Rod returned his attention back to the TV, I started to feel bad for the kid who took the brunt of that lesson. I could only imagine how Rod made him pay. It made me wish I had done the same thing to the bullies of my youth. I like to believe, however, they got their payback somewhere along the line, perhaps after running into someone like Rod, who wouldn't take their abuse.

CHAPTER ELEVEN

Ten Feet Tall and Bulletproof

—⊹⊱≡≷≡⊰⊹—

"Strength does not come from physical capacity.
It comes from indomitable will."
—Mahatma Gandhi

I am finally receiving that elusive spinal tap. Now that I'm back in the basement, I recall how Rod and I were left for dead here by that Spanish-speaking orderly. (Nothing, by the way, ever came from our mutiny in the basement yesterday; no one said a word about it.) Recalling the chaos that ensued—the big chase—helps me take my mind off my current predicament.

I'm lying facedown on an examining table, awaiting that unforgiving four-inch needle. This spinal tap is the next step on my path to remission. Every step gets me closer to my goal, but I still fear that needle. I continue wiggling my fingers and toes, hoping life as I know it doesn't end right here, in a darkened basement treatment room.

The permanency of this moment is overwhelming.

Throughout my entire life I've been able to find peace in one constant thing: there's always tomorrow. It's been my living epitaph:

no matter how bad things ever get, how many times I am kicked down, or how many regrets, failures, or falters I have in life, I can always close my bedroom door and, at worst, know tomorrow is a new day. I will always be guaranteed a clean slate, a new opportunity to redeem myself. Everything will always be all right come sunup, despite myself and despite whatever keeps getting me into these messes.

Lying here, I realize I have no such guarantee.

Although this is the most challenging moment I've ever been in, I try to remain calm. I try to take my mind off things. As the doctor prepares for the procedure, arranging his tools on a silver tray like a dentist, I scan the room.

I notice a monster-size machine directly above me. I ask the doctor what it is. It's a fluoroscopy monitor, sort of a "live" X-ray, he says. It will help him navigate his needle between the highly sensitive vertebrae of my lower spine. I'm sure that helps my odds, but I still feel like the naked guy on the board game Operation, with the look of horror and the giant red nose that buzzes whenever the player makes a wrong move with the tweezers, or in this case, needle.

As I continue to scan the room, Rod comes into view.

He's in a small room connected to this one. I can see him through a large pane of glass, pacing behind the technician who will handle the X-ray controls. Rod looks to be in deep thought. That's not unusual for him, but it's different this time—he's in some kind of a trance. With his hand to his chin, head pointed slightly to the floor, he looks like a heavyweight boxer alone in his dressing room before a fight, staring into a mirror—into his soul—to see what he can summon from inside to take with him to the ring. I imagine this was Rod's ritual before games.

Although I can only really guess what Rod did before walking down the Michigan Stadium tunnel—or any other stadium in the country, college or NFL—I don't need to guess what he did once the game started. Rod told me he would get so fired up after leading his team onto the field, he felt like he was invincible.

I've witnessed this intensity firsthand even though I've never seen Rod play football in my life. We were in my apartment one afternoon, having one of our daily conversations, many of which led to story ideas. We were always getting these ideas, maybe about a former teammate of Rod's I could write a story about for the *Ann Arbor News*, a profile piece. Or something I could pursue later in my career, like examining a trend in the NFL for a national magazine: a *Sports Illustrated* or *The Sporting News* or *ESPN The Magazine*.

Rod, of course, has his opinions on all that is the NFL: rules; game plans; tactics; and the behavior of athletes, coaches, owners, and fans. He often voiced them to me, and his comments were usually so interesting I would rush to my laptop, open a file, and type them down verbatim. I had to move my computer from my bedroom to the kitchen table for this very reason: it was a much shorter distance to run.

While watching ESPN's preview of the 2001 football season, we caught a highlight of an offensive lineman blocking an opponent below the knees to keep him from getting to the quarterback.

"He didn't need to chop that guy," Rod said. "He was beat, but he could have done something else. He could have rolled with him, pushed him to the outside, and let the quarterback run underneath. My coaches always told me to keep my hands up and stay square with the defender. That way they couldn't get by us like that guy did. I had a way of getting an upper hand so I didn't have to go chasing anybody or throw myself at a dude's knees to block him. That's dangerous."

Rod got so excited explaining his tactic that he decided to demonstrate it. He slid the coffee table out of the way, lowered himself into a three-point stance, and began counting off a play—right in my living room. I rushed to my laptop, wanting to record everything I saw.

"Hut, hut . . . *hut!*"

After the last *hut* left Rod's mouth, he lunged forward at the invisible opponent, meeting him at waist level. Rod stood him up, taking away his balance, then wildly swept his arm across the opponent's chest.

Rod snarled. He barked. He made indiscernible noises while shuffling his feet on the carpet, wrestling with the mach opponent. At the end, Rod kept him pinned to the carpet (a pancake move, where you lay your opponent flat). Then, as if Rod heard a whistle calling the play dead, he hopped to his feet and started bobbing up and down like a boxer after delivering a knockout blow.

"Yeah, yeah!" Rod shouted. "I'm ten feet tall and bulletproof. I fear *no* man."

I could feel the energy seeping from Rod's body. It sucked the air out of the room. I stopped typing and stared at him from the kitchen table.

Watching Rod bob up and down helped me visualize him on the field. I could see him there in uniform, a stadium full of people looking on. As the air continued to escape from the room, I came to the conclusion, with my fingers frozen on the keyboard, that Rod may not really be Superman, but he was the closest thing to the Man of Steel I'd ever seen.

I recall that intense image of Rod now, as the X-ray monitor turns on. While I look at my spine on the monitor, I can feel Rod's intensity. As that long needle inches closer to my lower back, and I feel the doctor's cold hands on me, I believe Superman is in the next room, pacing, ready to break through the glass should anything go wrong.

Rod, of course, is not Superman. He's only someone who's been blessed with size and strength, and has used those things to create something powerful, not bulletproof. He did this mostly on the football field, for as long and hard as he could. He did it until fate stepped in and sidelined him for good, turning him back into Clark Kent.

Come the end of Rod's football career, he didn't have those physical tools anymore, but he still had a strong heart. That's why Rod was able to earn his spot on that Ravens Super Bowl team, a position on the sideline given to him by their head coach, Brian Billick.

"Rod is a quality backup center," Billick said in an April 25, 2000, press release I found on the Ravens Web site, "and if he comes in here and works hard, he'll have a chance to contribute."

"Billick knew I was still a competitor, still a warrior," Rod told me during our first interview for his story. "He knew I still could help the team."

"I was a locker-room guy," Rod added proudly about his role on that team.

What always amazed me about Rod's stories is the thread of resilience in them. How he continued to improve as an athlete, as a leader, even after all those injuries—how he spent his final year from the sideline and never complained about it. The worst I'd ever see Rod do is watch some highlights on TV, see football players thrust their bodies at will, cut on a dime, and say, "Wouldn't that be nice," followed by a shake of the head and a prolonged sigh.

Clearly Rod wishes he had had a 13-year career instead of 13 surgeries, but that's the reality of it, and he's dealing with it. I wish I had that ability now.

It seems every time I build some momentum in life—graduate from college, get a girlfriend, find a career—I end up right back where I started. In this case, diagnosed with cancer—again. I feel like all of the lessons Rod taught me back in Michigan, along with all the good times we had there, have been wiped clean from my record. Like I'm starting all over again. I don't know if I can do it this time: start over. I've already committed too much of myself to my recent past to have the carpet pulled out from under me again.

Dealing with this constant frustration has placed a giant chip on my shoulder, one so big I can't see it anymore, like it's a part of me. It reminds me of a question I've asked myself most of my life: am I worthy of success?

I've seen glimpses of it—with my creativity, my resilience, and my sense of humor that Mom loves so much. Yet here I am, back in the hospital basement, not freelancing for major papers—like covering the Detroit Pistons against the Seattle SuperSonics for the *Seattle Post-Intelligencer*, my most recent gig. Not tooling around Ann Arbor with Rod, or growing as a person, a son, a college graduate. It makes me wonder whether there really is something special out there for me, something real, something permanent.

One thing I notice I haven't asked is why me?

Why me?

Why *not* me? This stuff's been happening to me my whole life. The only question I have now is: how long is it going to take to get past this?

Rod, I'm sure, felt the same way after all of his injuries. He used to tell me he'd say the same thing to the doctors after they informed him of the devastating news: a torn ACL; a separated shoulder; a broken clavicle, hand, foot, finger, toe. "Let's ride."

"Let's ride?" I asked Rod when he first told me this.

"Yep," he said. "Now that we know what the problem is, what are we going to do to fix it?"

Rod's mantra has always amazed me. What I also found amazing is that whenever Rod needed something fixed, it always got done. Even though he was carted out of half the stadiums in the country with injuries, he always returned to the game.

Now Rod is helping me do the same: return to the game—of life.

CHAPTER TWELVE

Radio Days

——— ⋈ ———

"We must not allow other people's
limited perceptions to define us."
—VIRGINIA SATIR

here's another reason I'm not asking "Why me?" or "Why am I back here again?" It's because I've known I had a problem for a long time. It's a relief, in a way, knowing what the big mystery is. Not that it's leukemia, of course, but that *something* has been keeping me tied to my living-room couch as if in shackles. That's where Rod often found me during his visits to my apartment: prone on the couch, napping.

I spent most of the latter part of 2001 on that couch. It was a funk I now realize was similar to my first year at Michigan, when the pressures of classes, social life, and my future and past all teamed up against me. It got to where I had to take advantage of the free psychiatric counseling offered to students. "Got Stress?" the pastel flyers stapled onto kiosks all over campus asked. "Come to counseling!"

The stress I had also affected me physically: it came with massive headaches. A doctor at the campus health center diagnosed them as "cluster headaches" because they came in bunches, two or three a day. I had to carry around little yellow pills he prescribed me to soothe them. These headaches left me curled up in a fetal position in my dorm room every night, sweating, panting, praying for the pain to end.

When it finally did, when the agony subsided, it was the greatest feeling in the world, better than any drug—an incomprehensible sense of relief. I wanted to climb mountains, soar over valleys, ask girls out for coffee I'd never had the nerve to talk to before.

When these headaches recently started up again (thankfully, they haven't been as bad: just one a day and nowhere near as incapacitating), I didn't even have the energy to clean up the empty pizza boxes and submarine sandwich wrappers on the coffee table in front of the couch. This was the mess from the previous night's dinner—leftovers of a meal I'd pick up after working late at the office.

"Did you sleep on the couch again?" Rod would say, shaking his head after he dropped by following his workouts at the building.

For a while, Rod blew off my laziness, thinking it must be part of my undisciplined upbringing. But Rod knew me better than that. He knew my goal in life was to be more than a slug. So he often marched past the mess on the table and headed to the balcony window behind the couch. He'd grab hold of the blinds and thrust them open, allowing a blinding midday sun to soak up the darkness in the living room.

"It's a beautiful day out there," Rod would say. "Get off your butt and do something. Go to the gym."

The gym? Rod might as well have been telling me to run the Michigan Stadium stairs—all 98 of them. Sure, he and his teammates used to do that—every day in the heat, up and down dozens of times until their legs were practically gone. But Rod is an athlete. I wasn't getting paid to be in shape like athletes do. This was my thinking. So without regret I just lay on the couch, gripping the cushions until Rod gave up trying to encourage me. I thought maybe later I'd break out the laptop and take some notes if we were to get into a discussion—that is, if I could have just thrown away that mess from my last meal, take a shower, and get ready. Forget it. I just rolled over.

One morning after Rod dropped by, I was able to pry myself off the couch after he issued his revelry call: I hit the floor and did some push-ups.

"I'll show him," I thought. I started to count them off, like he counted off that play he used at the line of scrimmage to gain an upper hand on his opponent . . . and managed just three. Three.

Rod's look of disgust said it all.

⋯ ⋈ ⋯

Despite my laziness, my friendship with Rod continued to grow—as did our creative pursuits. It made me think that maybe our friendship would last. I thought maybe I wasn't just a reporter Rod was kicking around town with, a companion to be cast away when the tides of life inevitably changed, but rather a true friend he was confiding in. It felt like I was, in some way, a teammate to him, just as important as those he'd had on the football field.

The team bond between us was never stronger—or revealed to me more entertainingly—than during Rod's weekday radio show on WTKA-AM: *SportsBeat*.

Owners and producers of the Ann Arbor station had wanted Rod on the air for a long time. I remember him talking about it when Arun and I hung out with him that first time in my apartment. The owners of the station must have been stalling—it was summer, after all, when everything slows down in town. But with football season quickly approaching, they finally decided to ask Rod to come in for an "interview."

That is what Rod called it, his meeting with them—an interview. To me, that'd be like sitting down with the girl of your dreams and asking her for a bio and references, inquiring where she sees herself in five years. Who cares as long is it's with you? Everyone in town knew Rod's credentials, his reputation as a warrior, and, most crucial to the business of talk-radio, his ability to gab.

I accompanied Rod to the interview, which took place one sunny weekday afternoon in late summer. Rod and I, along with his female lawyer friend, car-pooled to WTKA's studios at the Domino's Farm complex on the northeast end of town. Former WTKA owner, Tom Monaghan, used to own Domino's Pizza, hence the location.

The lawyer and I sat in a small waiting area near the front of the spacious office, reading magazines and talking about nothing in particular. Rod was back in a conference room with the producers and general manager of the station. Before he went back there, the producers and the GM came out to greet us. Joining them was Dennis Fithian, the host of *SportsBeat*, Rod's potential cohost.

Dennis was a talk-radio veteran, an affable guy—definitely not a shock jock—whom I'd listened to before. Like most media members, Dennis was not an athlete, but he had all the requirements to fit the sports talk radio persona: a good voice—throaty—along with a witty persona and an encyclopedic knowledge of sports. I knew he'd be a perfect fit for Rod's in-your-face style and firsthand insights into the world of athletics. They'd be the yin and yang of radio personalities.

As the lawyer and I continued to wait for Rod, he suddenly appeared from around the corner.

"What are you doing here?" I asked, as I closed the copy of *Sports Illustrated* I'd been flipping through. "You've been in there just 10 minutes."

Rod didn't answer. He just stretched his back and let out an "Ohhhhh, man."

I asked him again, "What's going on?"

This time, Rod smiled and extended his arm. His palm was turned up, like he was waiting for me to put something in it. I was as confused as the reporters who watched Rod rifle through his wallet at the press conference before the Michigan State game.

"I have 'em eating out the palm of my hand, bro," Rod said with a chuckle, his arm still extended.

Rod's smile filled the waiting room. It made me want to crack up. I managed to contain my laughter, however, and remain professional. Rod, meanwhile, told us nothing about the interview. He just slipped back into the conference room almost as soon as he had appeared from around the corner. A few minutes later, Dennis sidled into the waiting area.

After saying hello, Dennis stood in the middle of the room, looking around but focusing on nothing. I was waiting for him to say something, to give us a clue as to what was going on back there or why he had come out.

A moment later, Dennis walked off. Before turning the corner, he looked back.

"I hope it works out," he said. His fingers were crossed.

— ·— ≡♦≡ —· —

Rod got the job, to the delight of Dennis, me, and a ton of Michigan football fans, I'm sure. Once on the air, Rod proved he's the right man for the job. His banter with Dennis was lively and entertaining, and his interviews with high-profile coaches (many of whom stood across the sideline from Rod both in college and in the pros) were unlike any I'd ever heard before. They were candid, not bland or vanilla like you tend to hear on sports radio. Many of the coaches were getting ready for the season and openly shared their tactics, philosophies, and goals with Rod. It was like being in a team meeting, not at home listening to the radio.

At the same time, Rod's rapport with callers, as well as his ability to get to the bottom of any story, was uncanny. It was as if Rod was on a mission to present the truth, no matter how it came across on the air. In other words, his opinions and questions were never veiled. Especially when it came to conversations with callers. One exchange stands out.

The caller, a middle-aged man, insisted professional athletes' salaries should be made available to the public. He was adamant in his belief that the salaries pro athletes received were too extravagant and if they accepted them, they should also accept that fans wanted to know the figures. It seemed he wanted them reported in newspapers each morning next to the box scores and season statistics.

"Fans have the right to know the salaries," the caller said.

"The *right*?" Rod objected.

"Yeah. We pay your salaries. If it wasn't for us buying the tickets, there would be no games to play."

This issue—salaries—touched a nerve with Rod. I remember an incident at my apartment, when Arun's friends came over to meet Rod. They immediately asked him how much money he made in the NFL. I could sense a train wreck coming, judging by how agitated Rod became, how he blew off each question. Thankfully, Rod gave everyone the impression he wasn't interested in engaging in the conversation. Train wreck avoided.

This time, over the WTKA airwaves, Rod's caboose went careening off the track.

"Sir, what do you do for a living?" he asked the caller.

I stopped typing and waited for the caller to answer. I was sitting at my kitchen table in front of my trusty laptop. With so many good ideas for stories bandied about the show, I took lots of notes.

"I'm a lawyer," the caller said, less than enthusiastically, as if he hardly saw the relevance in such a question.

"I assume you live in Ann Arbor?" Rod inquired.

"Yes I do."

"What's your name?"

The man told Rod his name, first and last.

"Okay, sir, now let me ask you this: how much money do you make a year?" Silence followed. "How much do you pull in each year as a lawyer in Ann Arbor?" More dead air. "Did you hear me?" Rod asked. "I asked how much money you make a year. How much does it cost to take care of your family in this city?"

"I'm not going to tell you that," the caller said, breaking his boycott of words.

"Well then," Rod replied, "don't you think it should be the same for athletes too?"

Thinking Rod had put an end to this issue, I leaned back in my chair and waited for him to call me. A lot of times after Rod drove home a point on the radio, like he had just done, he'd give me a call—during the show. I'd be typing away and then suddenly interrupted by the phone. It would be Rod, calling me on his cell phone from the studio during a commercial break.

That's when I discovered I was more of a teammate to Rod than a friend. You can bet he didn't flip through his cell phone address book for just anyone during the two-minute breaks in the show, using up the valuable time he was supposed to be using to prepare for the next segment.

"Was that good?" Rod always asked when he called. His voice was usually muffled, like he was cupping his hand over the phone.

"How'd it sound?"

"Good," I'd tell him. "It's always good."

As I prepared for the phone to ring, I heard the caller start talking again. Apparently the segment wasn't over.

"But we're the *fans*," he stammered. "Without us, there would be no game. You play for us."

"We don't give a damn about you," Rod barked. "We play for our families. We play for the guy lined up next to us. And we play for the patch of grass under our feet. We don't even see you in the stands."

I knew Rod wasn't being entirely truthful. His point, instead, was that athletes are not simply show ponies to be paraded around stadiums for the amusement of the paying customers. It's just a job, like the fans themselves have (presumably). And athletes do respect the fans, but only those worthy of respect, such as those who look at athletes as people, not commodities they have to know every bit of personal information about.

As I continued typing, the show went into a commercial break. Within seconds, the phone rang.

"Did you hear that?"

"Heck yeah!"

It sounded like Rod was in the hallway this time. His voice was much louder than usual, not muted like it was when he talked to me from the booth.

"What'd you think?" Rod asked. "Did I break it down?"

I paused, wanting to frame my words perfectly, just like he did with the caller. Finally, I let them loose.

"To hell with what you don't have passion for!" I said, repeating the mantra Rod and I recently came up with to describe a situation just like this—a moment of ultimate conviction.

"To hell with what you don't have passion for," Rod repeated.

As Rod returned to the show and me to my typing, I wondered how many listeners Rod had just enlightened. I used to listen to sports talk radio in LA all the time, and never before had I heard such a powerful comment from an athlete. It's like Rod said during our first interview for his story: "People think football is a spectator sport, a hundred thousand people around you. But when those guys walk onto that field and you're 'this' close from your opponent's face, you think I'm thinking about that fanfare? Heck no."

CHAPTER THIRTEEN

Coldest Water in the Big Ten

<hr/>

"Tell me and I forget; show me and I remember;
involve me and I understand."
—UNKNOWN

Because of Rod's renewed visibility, he soon became sought after everywhere he went. Besides the radio show, he made Sunday night appearances on FOX News' Detroit affiliate, WDIV, on its weekend wrap-up show, *Sportsnight*. Rod added insights to the Detroit Lions' weekly performances, as well as those of the rest of the NFL teams. Rod was a natural on television (only for some reason, he appeared 10 pounds lighter on TV, not heavier).

Rod's opinions were as poignant and revealing as you'd hear during a sit-down interview with a head coach. He developed them after years of hard work at one of the top college football programs in the country. Maybe that's why Rod speaks about Michigan (not just Michigan football, but the school in general) with such pride. Michigan pride he calls it.

Having this pride has earned Rod the respect of his peers and coaches, from the time he was a student. It's the same, I've noticed, for other Michigan graduates, and not just athletes. Doctors, politicians, artists, even astronauts—including all three crewmembers of Apollo 15—give back to their alma mater. During their 1971 lunar mission, Apollo 15 commander David Scott and pilots Alfred Worden and James Irwin, carried a miniature University of Michigan flag in their spacecraft, then left a charter of the University of Michigan Alumni Club on the moon.

Even journalists get into the mix, albeit on the earthly level. Many prominent sportswriters at newspapers and other national media outlets are Michigan Daily alums—*Detroit Free Press* columnists Drew Sharp and Michael Rosenberg, along with former ESPN anchor, Rich Eisen, come to mind. Eisen, now a senior anchor for the NFL Network, is also a member of my fraternity: Pi Kappa Phi. He graduated as a *Daily* sports editor just a few years before I started at the paper. I wanted to be like him: successful in my craft so I could someday give back to my alma mater at the same level he has.

I believe I have some Michigan pride simply by being a graduate of the school. But I know that's not what Rod is talking about. I'm a Michigan man, but not a Michigan *Man* with a capital *M*. I still need a firsthand look at how other Michigan Men give back to their school before I can claim their company.

I got that look on September 22, 2001—the date of the first Michigan football game after 9/11.

·—· ≅◆≋ ·—·

The game against Western Michigan was more anticipated than ever, as it came on the heels of the terrorist attacks just 11 days earlier. Fans had planned to show up at Michigan Stadium as a sign of solidarity to deliver the message that Americans wouldn't back down to the enemy. Still, security was a major concern. All around the country, in fact, security was heightened as sporting events reconvened after more than a week of cancellations.

As usual, I wasn't planning to be at the game. I mostly covered high school events on Saturdays: track meets, soccer games, swimming and wrestling tournaments along with the occasional Michigan football game. But on this historic Saturday, because so many prep events were still being postponed or canceled altogether, I had the day off.

I had planned to watch the game on TV and cheer on the Wolverines from my living-room couch. I awoke on game day morning to the usual sounds of fall Saturdays in Ann Arbor: early arriving fans migrating toward Michigan Stadium and the visiting team's marching band practicing its routines on the fields outside Schembechler Hall. I stayed in bed much longer than usual, taking in the sounds, thinking it was the sweetest alarm clock I'd ever had.

Eventually, I lured myself out of bed with the thought of fixing a bowl of cereal. A few minutes later, I plopped on the couch and prepared to watch the pregame festivities. Before I did, I switched on the radio. Rod was set to appear on WTKA's *Roundtable*, a show that premiered before Michigan's season-opening win over Miami of Ohio a couple weeks prior.

As I dove into my cereal, waiting for the radio show to begin, the phone rang. It was Rod.

"You getting ready for the show?" I asked him, a mouthful of Apple Jacks slurring my words.

I could hear noise in the background. It sounded like traffic, not pre–radio show banter.

"What's up, bro?" Rod asked.

"Getting ready to listen to you."

I was still trying to make out the noise in the background when Rod said, "Get ready, I'm coming over."

Before I could ask what was going on, Rod hung up.

I put down my cereal and went to my bedroom to change. Before I could get ready, I heard the knock at the door. Rod seemed to be in a big hurry. I figured this because he didn't take a seat on the couch or fetch something to eat.

"C'mon, you ready?" he asked from the doorway.

"Not really. I haven't showered yet."

"That's OK. Let's go."

I was sure we'd be back soon from wherever it was we were going, so I threw on a tank top, shorts, flip-flops, and an old white visor with a blue *M* on the front. I thought we might just be going to meet up with some of Rod's friends at a tailgate party or to meander around the area, soaking up the excitement.

Shortly into our walk to the stadium, we ran into the Michigan marching band. Before each home game, the band members leave their rehearsal facility—Revelli Hall—a couple blocks from the stadium, already in formation. While playing "The Victors," Michigan's age-old fight song, fans flock to the musicians as they march onward toward impending victory.

"The band was always my favorite part of the games," Rod said as the musical convoy passed by. "Do you know they perform a private concert for the players before every season?"

"No," I said as the intoxicating words rang out around us:

> *Hail! to the victors, valiant.*
> *Hail! to the conqu'ring heroes.*
> *Hail! Hail! to Michigan*
> *The leaders and best.*

"Before every season, we'd sit in the stands and they'd perform for us," Rod said as we walked alongside the musicians. "They fired us up. They're as much a part of any victory as the players."

I remembered Rod used to play in the band, so I could understand his passion.

"The drums were always my favorite," he said.

"Didn't you play trumpet?"

"Yeah. But I like the power of the drums." Rod's hands waved in exaggerated motion, as if he was beating the bass drum himself. "Listen to that."

With this up-close view of the band, I could see the musicians' elaborate outfits much better than I ever had at the game. I focused on their maize-and-blue color guard–like uniform, as well as their decorative headgear: chinstraps, side buttons, front chain. I imagined this was probably the first time Rod had seen the band this close since his last game in 1996. (That first game of the season, against Miami-Ohio, Rod was in the radio booth on the other side of the stadium, so he couldn't have seen it then.)

Soon, Rod and I were snaking through the crowd of tailgaters, inching our way toward the players' entrance near the rear of the stadium. I wondered whether Rod had arranged some passes for us to get into the game. "Why else would we be walking over here?" I thought to myself.

Before arriving at the entrance, we become engulfed by a sea of fans, security personnel, and vendors. In the midst of this, Rod turned and instructed me to stay close behind him. When he turned back, I made eye contact with one of the police officers guarding the entrance to the locker room. I got nervous, shaky, like I did when I used to sneak into R-rated movies as a kid.

I realized Rod had no passes waiting for us, and I also knew there was no way we were getting past this security.

I remembered hearing on the radio that week about all the extra security at the game. There supposedly were more police officers (uniformed and plain-clothed) in and around the stadium than at the Super Bowl and Republican and Democratic national conventions combined. Fans were advised to arrive 90 minutes early to make it through two extra security checkpoints and to be in their seats on time for a special pregame ceremony.

As we approached the entrance, I braced myself for the unavoidable confrontation with the police officers. Just then, I experienced what I consider my first religious epiphany: the officers moved aside like the parting waters of the Red Sea.

They offered Rod a nod then let him—and me—through. So much for the extra security at the game.

My only explanation for the reason they allowed us to slip through the door and turn the corner into the Michigan locker room—the one with a sign on the door reading MICHIGAN FOOTBALL PLAYERS, COACHES, AND PERSONNEL ONLY—is that the officers must have thought Rod was a late-arriving player. He was wearing his dark-blue

T-shirt with MICHIGAN in yellow letters across the chest, the one that made me think he was still a student when we met. Whatever the reason, I quickly stopped worrying about it; I didn't want to miss a second of what was going on.

We strolled through the Michigan locker room, which was unbelievable. I was usually in the press box right about then, shuffling through pregame notes and loading up on hot dogs and popcorn. The room was empty as the players were already on the field for warmups. The locker room was littered with crumpled-up shirts, empty tape rolls, and crushed paper cups.

There were inspirational messages on the wall. I tried to read them, but we were walking too fast. Before I knew it, we hustled past the showers, through another door, and found ourselves at the top of the tunnel leading to the field. We were not alone.

Rod and I were standing beside the 240 members of the Michigan marching band. They were lined up in pairs, stretching the entire length of the tunnel, this cavernous downhill porthole that would drop them off at the 50-yard line. They appeared to be psyching themselves up for their performance.

Some of them played their instruments, limbering their fingers. Others stretched, touched their toes, and bent their backs. Some slapped the back of the musician in front of them. Still others screamed, their voices amplified by the powerful acoustics in the tunnel.

"See how pumped up they are?" Rod said, nudging me. "And that's just the band members." Rod said nothing else, but I knew what he was suggesting: imagine how the *players* pump themselves up.

Soon, the band members walked down the tunnel and onto the field for their pregame performance. Rod and I followed them. As we neared the base of the tunnel, I had another religious experience—the press box and upper rows of the stadium slowly lowered from the sky as if on pulleys from heaven (an image created by the long canopy at the end of the tunnel, which camouflages the sky until you get closer to the field).

The rest of the crowd appeared against a blue-sky backdrop. There was a world of fans around us, all awash in maize and blue, with a speckle of brown and yellow in the end zone (Western fans). We were encased by this mass of humanity, protected. We were not going anywhere, it appeared, which is how the players must have felt: like gladiators. Rod had always referred to them as that—modern-day gladiators.

Right near us by the tunnel's entrance, I saw a group of Michigan players, a dozen or so. I watched them and realized Rod was right: the band members do a decent job of psyching themselves up for the game, but the players take it to a different level, a startling level.

Some of them hopped up and down in rhythm. Others butted helmets; hit each others' shoulder pads, chest; and crack their necks. I could see the eyes of a few of them through the slits in their facemask bars—like wolves on the prowl. An offensive lineman I recognized, Jonathan Goodwin, was frothing at the mouth. Foam—actually pouring through his helmet, onto his jersey.

While taking in the shocking sight, I noticed another player— shorter but equally as intense as Goodwin. He was whipping his head around, his helmet making him look like a giant Michigan football bobble-head doll. He noticed Rod standing next to me, and stopped cold.

"Hey, Rod," the player said in a boyish tone. "How's it going?"

"Good," Rod said, stepping closer to him.

I'd already taken a step back, giving the players a wide berth in case they decided to get really out of control. Rod shook hands with the guy. He was right next to the gladiators, as if he was about to run onto the field himself. Some of the others stopped their ritual and said hello to Rod.

"Go get 'em boys," Rod said, then stepped back toward me.

"We will, Rod," the diminutive one said, then hopped back into the group and started whipping his head into a fury.

I'd been in that historic stadium more than a dozen times before— in the stands, in the press box, even on the field. (After the game, reporters walk up the tunnel behind the players to conduct their postgame interviews in the media room.) But I'd never been in it like that: on the field, minutes before the game, a crowd of 109,837 already in their seats and making their presence known. And with the significance of 9/11 still hovering over us (and an unprecedented five-mile no-fly zone around the stadium), it was like nothing I'd ever experienced.

A few minutes later, Rod and I ran into Coach Schembechler. We were walking to Michigan's side of the field, and we saw him standing in the north end zone. He was about to be honored along with players from one of his Big Ten championship teams from the '70s. I shook hands with a few of the players, then Coach Schembechler, who smiled at me. He was wearing his trademark dark glasses and oversized *M* cap, looking like a grizzled Army general.

As Coach Schembechler and I chatted, I noticed the marching band forming a giant block *M* at midfield. They marched toward us in formation while playing "The Victors." I felt a breeze on my face. Surreal.

Rod and I continued walking to the Michigan sideline. As we did, I looked up in the stands and noticed all the students in their usual sections, between the 15-yard line and the back of the end zone. I tried to see whether I recognized any of them—I didn't. It was just row upon row upon row of faces. They were endless.

"See that girl right there?" Rod said, pointing five or six rows up.

"No. Where?"

"That blonde girl right there—in the pink sweatshirt."

"Yeah, I see her now."

"After the game, we would just point to her, and that would be that."

"What do you mean?"

"She'd come down to the railing, and we'd tell her where our party was going to be later. And that was all we needed to do."

"You're kidding."

"Nope. Any girl we wanted."

Before I could think about this incredible fringe benefit of playing Division I football, Rod led me to the Michigan bench. He took a seat, leaned back, and started soaking up the scene. I joined him. I couldn't believe we were actually sitting on the Michigan bench. As the band wrapped up its performance, Rod and I clapped along with the rest of the stadium. Rod clapped harder than me, as if he really wanted the band to hear him.

When the musicians took their place in the stands—where they would play "The Victors" every time Michigan scored—Rod and I stood up, along with the players, for the singing of "The Star-Spangled Banner." Rod told me this was the first time the players would be on the field for the national anthem. Usually they were in the locker room. But in respect to the victims of 9/11, the players and coaches would be there with us, looking up at the American flags waving from the upper bowl of the stadium. This was where the flags of the Big Ten teams used to be. The Stars and Stripes would stay up the whole year, a team assistant nearby told us. And to our left, unfurling across the field, was a colossal American flag, the biggest I'd ever seen. It stretched across half the field.

After the emotional ceremony, which included a moment of silence and a flyover by a trio of Air Force jets, Rod and I sat back on the bench with the players. We were just off to the side of the action, but not so far we couldn't hear the players talking with their position coaches. The defensive unit was right near us, discussing early adjustments with its coaches after coming off the field following the first series of the game.

"You're doin' good out there, boys," Rod said, mimicking the coach. "Just fill those gaps, stick to your man. Watch for those sweeps."

Sweat, I noticed, was pouring down the players' heads.

"It must be hot on the field," I said.

"Shoot, it's hot right here," Rod responded as he grabbed one of the players' towels and wiped the sweat off his arms and head. "I'll get us some water."

Rod whistled to the water boy, who was coming off the field after a timeout.

The water boy was holding an eight-pack of those green Gatorade bottles I always see on TV. He handed one to Rod.

"Thanks," Rod said as he popped the top off and squirted a generous amount of water down his throat. Rod passed the bottle to me. I took a sip, a much smaller one than Rod. The water was cold—ice cold. It was so cold it almost hurt to drink it.

"Damn, this is cold," I said.

"That's right," Rod replied, taking the bottle back.

"See," he said after downing another gulp, "even the dude carrying the water at Michigan takes pride in what he does."

This is when I began to understand what Michigan pride was all about. It was not just about playing in the NFL, like Rod and A-Train and Woodson did, or becoming a famous playwright, like Henry Miller, or flying to the moon, like the Apollo 15 astronauts. It was simply about doing your job, no matter what it is—like that water boy.

I took a close look at him: he looked like a student. He flashed a smile that said "pride, honor, joy."

"Coldest water in the Big Ten," the kid said. He was holding the rack of eight tight to his side, head upright, like a Marine.

Rod gulped down more water.

"That's why Michigan is a championship contender every year," Rod said, handing me the bottle. "Everybody here at Michigan are dawgs."

At halftime, the parking lot was still buzzing with tailgaters. They were watching the game on small televisions, some roasting sausages on portable barbecues and dishing potato salad onto paper plates. I suddenly got hungry.

"Let's go home and eat," I said to Rod.

"Yep," was all he replied.

We left the game early because we decided we had gotten the gist of the excitement. We could still hear the cheers from the stadium as we neared the practice fields by my apartment, where Western's band had been rehearsing a couple hours earlier. There we saw, walking toward us, a recruit getting a tour of campus from a team representative. The two of them stopped just before passing us. (I was wondering why the recruit wasn't at the game, but I didn't say anything about it.)

"Rod, how's it going?" the rep asked, then introduced the player: a big, burly kid from Texas.

"Rod was team captain and MVP of the '96 squad; first-team All-American . . . and All–Big Ten, right, Rod?"

Rod nodded his head.

"And he won the Super Bowl with the Ravens."

After sharing that information, the rep flashed a toothy smile at the player as if to suggest, "See, you too can be a Super Bowl champion if you just go to Michigan."

I was proud to stand back and watch the encounter between a former player an up-and-coming one, the torch of knowledge being passed. But somehow, the exchange was bobbled, and the torch fell to the ground.

"You a lineman?" Rod asked as he gripped the player's hand. "You a big man?"

The player nodded shyly.

Rod asked again, "You a big man?"

Again the nod.

Confused, I could sense some aggravation in Rod's voice, see some concern on the tour guide's face.

"You a big man?" Rod repeated, still gripping the player's hand. "Then why don't you shake hands like a man? Grab hold of my hand, son. You supposed to be a lineman, right? A big dog." The player must have given Rod a wet-noodle handshake—if that's possible. This kid was the size of a four-door Chevy.

The recruit continued to give a dopey smile, nod his head. Rod finally let go of his hand and said so long to the team assistant, but not to the player.

"I'll check you at the building later," Rod said as he and I walked off.

"He's from Texas?" Rod asked me a few moments later.

"That's what I heard."

"Let him stay in Texas. We don't want him at Michigan."

While thinking about that, I realized I'd completely forgotten to ask Rod why he wasn't on the radio before the game. At that point, I didn't really care. I think I learned more from what Rod showed me about the Michigan football team than I would have by listening to him talk about it for an hour.

＊＋ ＝＊＝ ＋＊

I gained a lot from that encounter with the recruit. He had a golden opportunity to ask Rod anything about Michigan, college in general, or the NFL. With everything Rod had already told me, I'm sure he would have broken it down for the player, told him anything he wanted to hear. And what did the recruit do? He gave Rod the cold fish!

That disturbed me. I wondered how someone of such physical talent could throw away an opportunity like that. Funny thing is, I could actually relate to him because I'd done just the same before—walked away from advice, from knowledge. I'd done it so many times in my life, I didn't want to even think about making that costly mistake again.

Thus, despite my laziness in recent weeks, I decided to make it a point to always greet opportunity like a man—if only to shake hands like one.

CHAPTER FOURTEEN

Put It on the Table

"If you have a chance to make things better and you don't,
you're wasting your time on this earth."
—ROBERTO CLEMENTE

I eventually learned why Rod hadn't gone on the air before
that first game after 9/11. He'd been having a dispute with the
station's producers. They'd been giving him mixed messages
about his role at WTKA, specifically over what it would be for those
game day–morning telecasts. They stopped communicating with Rod,
which he's always said is the first thing that can ruin a good team.

Still, Rod continued to do his weekday afternoon show and tended
to his car-customizing company. Yet he managed to drop by 1313
nearly every day.

While our conversations continued, so did our adventures. And
traveling around town gave Rod more chances to introduce me to
people—friends of his, former teammates, business partners. Seeing
him interact with them also allowed me to learn more about Rod,
namely the skills he possessed that extended beyond the football field.

Rod had a unique way of making things happen. He was expeditious, efficient, and always entertaining. Not only could he impress a giggling coed—"You're as cute as a button," he'd say as she got a close-up view of the ring—but he could also talk the utility belt off a female Ann Arbor police officer (figuratively speaking, of course). On the other hand, I could say the same thing to an armed, bleach-blonde cop—"Hey sweetie, you're looking good in that uniform"—and would be in handcuffs before I could finish the sentence.

What also impressed me was Rod's business savvy and how he always kept me in the loop during our daily encounters with the town's elite. Rod never hesitated to pull me into the fray and introduce me to someone he knew. "This is my boy," he sometimes said when introducing me to a storeowner he knew at the local mall, Briarwood.

The owner of Out the Door clothing was thinking about advertising his store on Rod's show. I told him the benefits of that. I explained the show's demographics and how he couldn't go wrong going into business with Rod. "He'll take care of you," I said. "Believe me."

Sometimes when Rod introduced me to someone, he would say, "This is my ace, my No. 1," which I liked even more. He called me that when we met up with a former Michigan teammate of his, Chuck Winters, who was playing with the Arena Football League's Detroit Fury. Chuck and Rod twice came over to my apartment, where we ordered food and drank beers. I always felt relaxed and laid-back in their presence, like I did when Rod and Jamie and I first hung out. It was like I was on par with these big-time athletes. If only my elder coworkers could have seen me then.

⚊ ≼✦≽ ⚊

As I continued to soak up Rod's knowledge, I began to see how passionately he distributed it—and to how many people. I first noticed this when we met up with a group of friends at a local pizza joint, Cottage Inn, one Friday night. They were mostly friends of Rod's and friends they brought to the party. I didn't know many of them, and I presumed Rod didn't either. Still, he had no problem keeping the entire group rapt during the course of the evening.

Rod talked very little about football, yet everyone still hung on his every word. They were enthralled with his insights on current events, culture, politics, or whatever topic he introduced. They all laughed at his stories, his self-deprecating humor, and his friendly jabs at people at the table who, let's say, were a little fashion challenged.

Rod thinks he has the style sense to put together an outfit as daring as Tommy Hilfiger. He's also never afraid to point out somebody else's inability to do the same, not in a vindictive kind of way, but merely in a boy scout–like, need-to-provide-the-facts manner. Even I wasn't exempt from this. I remember Rod's reaction when I showed up wearing the blue tennis shoes Nana bought me during my latest trip to Palm Springs.

"What's wrong with the shoes?" I asked Rod.

"They're blue," he said.

"So what? Mark Rosen [Michigan's head volleyball coach] just gave me a compliment on them. He said, 'Nice blue shoes—Michigan's colors.'"

"Bro, Rosen should stick to volleyball. *Nobody* wears blue shoes. You never would have survived in a football locker room. Those dudes would have ripped you apart. That's how I learned how to dress. Or else I never would have heard the end of it."

Luckily, on the night of the pizza party, I didn't look too bad— khaki shorts; flip-flops; one-color T-shirt, earth tone. Just as I began to marvel at my summery attire and realize the strides I'd made since meeting Rod, all those fashion tips I absorbed, the party wound down. It was closing in on 12. As everyone got up, a guy from across the table announced he needed a ride home and asked someone to take him.

Everyone was silent, so Rod volunteered.

"Thanks, man," the fellow said. "I live right near campus." Rod and I had never met the guy. He didn't say much during the evening as I recall.

"No problem," Rod said.

During the midnight drive through downtown Ann Arbor, our

passenger supplied directions from the backseat. I was so tired, I just wanted to get home, so I didn't say much on the ride. I barely ate at the restaurant, in fact, choosing instead to pick at everyone else's plates. Rod took exception with that and let me know about it. "Order your own food," he said. "You don't do that to people."

Despite the late hour, Rod continued being the lively host. He talked to our passenger, asking him what he did for a living, where he was from. Honestly, I didn't know how Rod could do it. By the time we arrived at the guy's apartment, I was nearly passed out.

Still, I was alert enough to hear him thank Rod. Not for the ride, but the entire evening.

"It's really cool you were there," he said as he unbuckled and prepared to climb out of the truck. "You make it a great time."

Rod whipped his head around.

"*You* made it a good time," he said, staring the guy right in the eye. "Without you, it wouldn't have been the same."

I was suddenly jarred awake. I turned around. The guy was aglow in the backseat. After hopping out of the cab, he practically floated across the street and up the stairs to his apartment. I think I know why.

It had to do with what Rod has always told me: any group's success is contingent on all of its members, not just in athletics, but also at pizza parties, I presumed. The guy, I'm sure, now realized Rod wasn't up on a pedestal simply because he was a football player. Instead, we were all equal at that table. That fellow was right there with Rod, along with me and everyone else. That's why he heard all those impassioned and entertaining words Rod delivered. Without all of us, Rod wouldn't have had anyone to tell those words to. If anything, we inspired *him* just by being there to listen.

Taking Rod's lead, I have started to say the same thing whenever someone tells me that I somehow made an occasion a good time, a better time, just by being there.

"*You* made it that way," I tell them, my response hardly original. "Without you, it wouldn't have been the same."

The next day at work, I saw another example of Rod's unselfishness, of his desire and ability to help somebody. This time, it was a teammate.

While walking out of the newsroom at the end of my shift, I came across a 1996 Michigan football media guide. Rod was on the cover, along with a pair of Ohio State defensive linemen. With his arms outstretched, and his back to the players—somehow Rod got turned around on the play—Rod was doing everything he could to keep the rush of Buckeyes away from his quarterback.

I took a closer look. Rod's fingers, mangled and wrapped in tape, were stretched as far as they could, every inch the difference between success and failure, between his quarterback throwing for a first down, a touchdown, or scrambling for a big gain. Rod was putting his teammates on his shoulders, carrying them to victory as best he could.

When I mentioned the media guide to Rod the next time I saw him, reminding him about the cover—he actually had forgotten he was on it—he said he was really falling down in that picture.

"They were holding me up," he said, his arms loosely outstretched, a far cry from their iron-bar look in the photo. Rod laughed, letting me in on his joke.

"No they weren't," he added, his tone now serious.

I once heard Terry Bradshaw, the Pittsburgh Steelers' Hall of Fame quarterback, say, "You may lose with me, but you'll never win without me."

Bradshaw, who has four Super Bowl rings, was asked during an interview on ESPN Classic to sum up his career as a gritty, iron-jawed product of the South (Louisiana State University). Rod, even with just one ring to his credit, can say the same thing, I reckon. Teams needed someone who could play like Rod if they wanted a chance to win.

My good fortune to have Rod on my team always gave me a proud feeling. And when I was writing good stories at work and taking care of affairs in other areas of my life, I was able to enjoy our friendship. But when I wasn't, when I succumbed to the rigors of my job, failed to turn in good stories, and put forth a less-than-quality effort to the process, I felt guilty, like I wasn't living up to Rod's powerful example.

Eventually, I started making excuses for my half-hearted effort.

I often worked late at the office, until one or two in the morning. And after those exhausting desk shifts, by the time I got home and wound down, I wouldn't fall asleep until *SportsCenter*'s early a.m. repeat. And if I got a vision, some kind of story idea, I'd have to leave my warm bed, dash to my laptop, and write it down.

"Just type a few things," I would tell myself, "then go back to sleep." Yet inevitably, a marathon writing session awaited. When that happened, more times than not, I wouldn't get to bed until *Today*'s opening segment.

The time came, after months of this draining schedule, when I simply could not keep up with Rod's expectations for me. Although I appreciated what he was doing to help me—the direction he gave me, the instructions, the encouragement—the bar was set too high. When that happened, I started to search for solace in the cushions of my couch. Rod still tried to detach me from them, day after day, week after week, until it was time for my annual trip home for the holidays.

I'd been taking mid-December vacations—first to LA to visit Mom, then to Sun City West, Arizona, to visit my dad and stepmother, Geri—since I moved to Michigan. I looked forward to the trips: they were rare occasions to reconnect with my youth, even if only to remind me of how unsatisfactory it was and of how far I'd come since then.

Now, for some unexplained reason, I was on edge whenever I thought about the trip. It felt like my back was to the wall, but I had no idea why. This made minor annoyances that normally inspired me to curl up on the couch, dreaming of better days, become major irritations. I couldn't relax, I couldn't dream. I couldn't do anything. And I paid little attention to the clues that surfaced that might have tipped me off to the cause of this turmoil.

The strange lumps on my neck, for instance, just below my ears. Or the hemorrhoid that blindsided me, a rare pain in the butt I hadn't felt since those late nights in the library, studying for my economics exams. And the odd irritation in my groin when I stepped in and out of my low-riding car. I hadn't told anybody about those things. That was how I was trained: keep your problems to yourself.

That became harder to do with Rod always on my back, always wanting to know what was going on with me. In addition to that, I had other problems. One involved a coworker who had become as painful as that hemorrhoid. My issue with him started when I covered a high-school soccer match in East Lansing. The field was an hour northwest of Ann Arbor, right near Michigan State's campus. Rod and I had planned to meet up with some friends after the game back in Ann Arbor.

In my rush to leave the field after I finished my interviews, I forgot to get some information into the story, some meaningless agate (statistics, such as shots on goals, penalties, etc.). So I called my coworker at the paper and asked him to call the coach—we had a list of coaches' home and cell numbers at the office—and get the information for me. He assured me he would, and I assumed the oversight would be kept between us.

Next day in the office, my boss asked me why I hadn't gotten the agate into the story. I was dumbfounded my coworker would do that to me. I knew I wasn't part of the gang around the office, but I had thought there was some type of professional courtesy in this business. I tried to put that coworker out of my mind, but I couldn't. I'd never felt more betrayed in a workplace environment. (Well, other than when I was booted out of Sony.)

Just a couple days before my trip to LA, Rod and I were preparing lunch in my apartment when the conversation shifted from what to watch on TV—ESPN or a movie—to my job. I thought of that coworker and immediately shut down. This triggered Rod's "Spidey sense." He actually calls it that.

ABOVE: Steve in 1995, playing bass in the band Hyperchild at the F.M. Station in Hollywood, California.

BELOW: Steve and his mom, Paula, at a family wedding in Minneapolis, Minnesota.

RIGHT:
Rod (64) in his first
year with the Cincinnati
Bengals, 1997. Rod was
the second center
selected in the 1997
NFL Draft, in the
third round.

LEFT:
After being turned around on this
play at Michigan Stadium in 1995,
Rod stalls a pair of Ohio State
Buckeye defensive linemen.
The picture graced the Michigan
football media guide the following
season and illustrates Rod's
dedication as a teammate and
his resilience as a competitor.
Photo courtesy of Ronald J. Heys

ABOVE: Rod with some of his fellow fifth-year seniors prior to the 1997 Outback
Bowl in Tampa, Florida. (Clockwise starting from left—first standing player):
Thomas Guynes (75); Rod Payne (52); Jarrett Irons (37); Mark Bolach (89);
Remy Hamilton (19); Mike Vanderbeek (45); Paul Peristeris (99); Harold Goodwin;
Woodrow Hankins (23); Steve King (27).

LEFT: Steve at the *Ann Arbor News* sports department in 1999, while still a student at the University of Michigan. Note the historic Atex computer system, the so-called green screen.

ABOVE: Steve with Tom Brady in August 2000, then a fourth-string quarterback for the New England Patriots. Photo taken after a Patriots–Detroit Lions game at the Pontiac Silverdome, while Steve was working for the *Ann Arbor News*. Tom and Steve were classmates at the University of Michigan, graduating in 2000.

ABOVE: Rod and Steve (foreground left) with friends at an Ann Arbor restaurant in September 2002, during Steve's first trip back to Michigan following his 10 months of treatment in Los Angeles.

RIGHT:
Steve and Dr. David Snyder at the City of Hope in March 2002. Dr. Snyder, a native of Boston, helped calm Steve down while he waited for a transplant by discussing Boston sports.

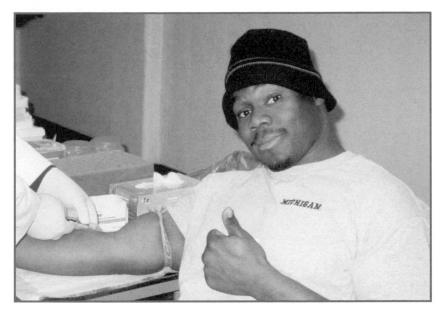

ABOVE: Rod giving blood for Steve at a bone marrow drive put on by the *Ann Arbor News*. Ninety of Steve and Rod's coworkers and friends came to the downtown building to give blood. None of them were a match for Steve, but now they're in the national marrow list and can possibly help someone else.

RIGHT: Steve with his first nurse at City of Hope in early May 2002, right before his bone marrow transplant. Barring complications, the procedure takes a month to complete and requires many kinds of chemotherapy, intravenous nutrients, and other medicines, each of which are connected to a machine on his IV pole.

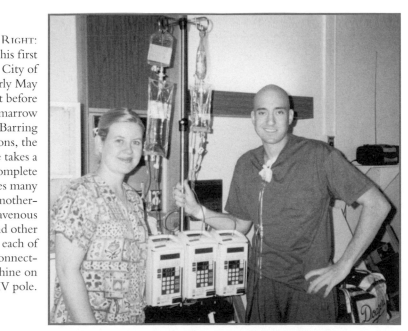

LEFT: Steve's mom, Paula, helping him prepare for his bone marrow transplant in the "Hope Village," the City of Hope's on-site family living quarters. Pre-chemotherapy treatments are needed for the transplant and are performed by a caregiver of the patient.

BELOW: Steve with his mom and grandmother, Pearl (right), in the City of Hope bone marrow ward on May 4, 2002, the day of his bone marrow transplant. Anyone in Steve's room had to wear a mask because his immune system had to be reduced to zero to accept the donor's blood.

ABOVE: Jessica (Steve's girlfriend), Steve, and Rod, in September 2002, during Steve's first trip back to Michigan following his 10 months of treatment in Los Angeles.

LEFT:
Steve and his bone marrow transplant donor, Annette Lechler, at the City of Hope's annual bone marrow survivors reunion in April 2005. Annette was flown to Duarte, California, from her home in Dottinger, Germany. It was the first time the two met.

LEFT: Steve in Fall 2004 in the Arizona Diamondbacks dugout before a game at Bank One Ballpark (now Chase Field) in Phoenix, working for the *Arizona Daily Sun*.

ABOVE: Steve in the press box at Sun Devil Stadium before a 2004 Arizona Cardinals game as a reporter at the *Arizona Daily Sun*.

"What's wrong?" Rod said as he took a seat on the couch, setting the sandwich he had just made on the long wooden coffee table in front of him.

"Nothing." I got up from the couch and headed to the kitchen to prepare my own sandwich.

"What's going on?" Rod said, his mouth full of wheat bread, lettuce, and turkey slices. Rod's tone was casual. He took another bite of his sandwich. He seemed indifferent to whether he actually found out what was bothering me or not.

"Nothing, I told you." Of course I was lying, thinking what a clown that coworker had been to go behind my back like that. "Everything's cool," I said.

I resolved to make my sandwich, thinking I'd said enough to convince Rod he should just change the subject. Still, I offered one more thing, just to make sure.

"I got everything under control," I said. This is what I've always done to blow off anyone who tried to patronize me by asking whether I had a problem. After all, what does anyone else care?

All those years of coming home to an empty apartment, no one asked me if I had a problem then. No one ever asked if I needed to talk about anything (like getting beat up at school every day, in one way or another, sometimes by my own friends). They didn't care much back then, so why should they care now?

As predicted, Rod didn't ask again. He just set his sandwich on his plate and put it on the coffee table. The table was cluttered with car magazines Rod brought over, dishes from breakfast, keys, newspapers, a pair of scissors I clipped my stories out of the paper with, and an inkpad I used to stamp the date on them for my portfolio. Rod cocked his arm back and thrust it clear across the table, sending everything flying across the room like shrapnel. It all smashed into the wall with a crash.

I froze in my steps. My eyes darted toward the debris, which was still settling in the corner of the apartment. I focused on it, allowing the sight—and the message it sent—to sink in. I looked back at Rod. He was staring at me with daggers in his eyes while stabbing his finger at the now-empty coffee table.

"Put it on the table," Rod said, punctuating each word with a stab that made a loud thump. "C'mon, bro. Just *put* . . . it *on* . . . the *table*."

Rod, I realized, wasn't going to let go of the subject. There was no way I was going to blow him off like I'd done to everyone else who dared try to break through the protective wall I built around myself so long ago.

As Rod continued to stab at that table, my jaw dropped—along with my defenses—and I started to explain my problem. As I did, I actually felt better—just by talking about it.

After Rod listened to what I had to say, he gave me advice on how to handle my coworker. It's simple, he said, "Confront him. Show him you won't tolerate that crap."

For the record, I was going to just avoid him, which is how I'd always handled punks like him.

"Next time you see him," Rod added, "just say, 'Why'd you play me like that?'"

Rod spoke calmly, clearly, as if he hadn't just turned my apartment into World War III, while I remained shocked over the mess crashing into the wall. While I continued to stare at the rubble, Rod lifted himself off the couch and started to clean up. I joined in.

As we picked up the pieces of that moment—literally and figuratively—I thought about when I'd be able to apply Rod's advice. I was excited to put his plan into action, to confront my coworker, ask him why he played me like that. I at least owed Rod that—to try, to show him I appreciated the work he just put in eliminating my deep-rooted problem.

Turns out, I never got the chance.

CHAPTER FIFTEEN

Close the Blinds!

—— ⚎ ——

"It is a rough road that leads to the heights of greatness."
—Seneca

I could tell something was wrong. While waiting for Rod to drop by my apartment and take me to the airport, I began to feel nervous, uneasy about the trip. I wanted to call Mom and tell her I was not coming home: there'd been a change of plans. But of course, I couldn't. This was my annual trip home. I'd have disappointed Mom and Dad if I hadn't seen them. The tickets were booked, my vacation had been approved for months, and I would be on the flight. Plus, I somehow knew everything would be all right.

Despite my anxiety, it was not hard to convince myself of this: I mean, I was *always* all right.

An hour later, as Rod pulled my Eclipse up to the curb at Detroit Metro Airport, I made it a mission to use this trip to my advantage. I was going to regroup while in LA, rest up, then come back to Michigan strong and start to show Rod that the time he'd spent with me was not spent in vain. I determined to rise up to his daily challenges, get off the couch—do anything to show him I was still the teammate he saw in me. This despite how I handled things with that coworker. I never did confront him, like Rod told me to. I didn't see him in the office before I left for my vacation, so I just sent him an e-mail explaining my grievance. I decided to deal with him when I got back.

As I hugged Rod good-bye at the curb and then watched him drive off in my car, I promised myself there would be no more excuses for my laziness.

"When I return home," I said while walking through the sliding glass doors into the terminal, "things are going to be different."

<hr />

Everything went well during my week in LA. Mom worked her usual nine-hour shift at the doctor's office, and I spent most of each day rummaging through my old bedroom, unearthing some of those rare artifacts from my past. I found old records and CDs, pictures of me with the bands (long hair, leather chaps, cowboy boots), and the commemorative newspapers I used to collect, including all 16 issues of the *Los Angeles Times* when LA hosted the Olympics in 1984.

At night, Mom and I hung out. We went to Los Angeles Dodger baseball games, out to dinner, to the movies. On the weekend, we made the same two-hour drive to Palm Springs to visit Nana that we'd made all my life.

I called Rod from PS, as the locals refer to their desert home, and told him the vacation was going fine: "We shopped for clothes today, had dinner at a fancy restaurant; I had prime rib. In a couple days I'll be in Arizona, visiting my dad and stepmother, then home."

"Cool," Rod said. "We have to get back to work." A new calendar year was upon us, 2002, and I was excited about the possibilities. This was to be my first trip back to Michigan with a lot to look forward to—my friendship with Rod being the biggest, as well as all of our plans: the articles, books, and businesses, even a production company we wanted to start up. With our contacts, we felt anything was possible.

"The only difference between them and us," Rod said when we watched Jay-Z or other rappers doing their thing in music, film, clothing, and everywhere else, "is that they're doing it and we're not."

I looked forward to getting back to work, furthering my journalism career. I had just covered my first regular-season professional sporting event—that Pistons-Sonics game for the *Seattle P-I*—and I anticipated more freelance gigs like that. Most of all, I looked forward to keeping the promise I had made to myself outside the departure terminal at Detroit Metro—to get up off the couch and start being a teammate instead of an observer in life. Rod always had another way to put that. He knew by heart a poem by Theodore Roosevelt, which he found in his playbook at Michigan every year.

"It is not the critic who counts," he would quote, "not the man who points out how the strong man stumbles, or where the doer of deeds could have done them better. The credit belongs to the man who is actually in the arena, whose face is marred by dust and sweat and blood; who strives valiantly . . . who at best knows in the end the triumph of high achievement; and who at the worst, if he fails, at least fails while daring greatly so that his place shall never be with those cold and timid souls who know neither victory nor defeat."

Following our trip to PS, Mom and I drove to an upscale restaurant in the San Fernando Valley. My cousin, George, invited us to a special brunch. His wife, Terry, and teenage daughter, Raquel, would also be there. This was my big sendoff to Arizona, where Dad and Geri moved from the cold of Minnesota roughly six years earlier: retirement in all its glory, no kids around, nothing but elderly people and slow drivers.

At the restaurant, we indulged on the fare that normally lines long buffet tables. I always ate the same things at these events: extra thick sausages, raw oysters, California rolls, scrambled eggs for color, water, coffee, juice, and anything else I could fit on my plate as I made my way back to the table. Seated at the corner of the table, I unfolded my cloth napkin and began to eat. Before the first bite even settled—a combination of eggs and a piece of California roll—I felt a piercing chill shoot through my body. It was more like a sting, actually. I set down my fork and took a deep breath.

A moment later, I picked my fork up again. I cut a piece of sausage, followed it up with a scoop of eggs, and washed it down with a drink of water. That was a bad idea. My stomach took a nosedive.

I started to get worried. This was just too odd. "It can't be the food, can it?" I wondered.

I looked around and noticed where we were sitting: at a table right by a tall window, where the unrelenting San Fernando Valley sun was pouring over us like a cascade of used frying grease. (I remembered the feeling from when I worked at Burger King in Minnesota and had to empty the black muck from the French fry machine each shift.) The sun washed out everything around us: the yellow in the eggs and my sense of control over the situation, along with any hope that the rest of my vacation would be enjoyable.

My first thought was to try to tough it out—then to bail out, then decided I was overreacting. Everyone else seemed to be enjoying the meal.

George was on the opposite side of the table, between Terry and Raquel. They all chewed on giant crab legs as George gave us his prediction for who would play in the upcoming Super Bowl, along with how the Lakers, our favorite basketball team, would do that year. Mom, seated next to me, picked delicately at her egg-white omelet. They were all laughing, talking, enjoying themselves. I tried to participate, but I couldn't. I managed to smile, but I wanted to run like hell.

Next time the waiter came to the table, I asked him to close the blinds. As he leaned over the table to reach them, I watched his grease-stained tie settle on the white tablecloth, which for whatever reason made me feel sick. He appeared to have trouble closing the blinds.

"They're broken," he said, then poured us some water.

Broken? What does he mean broken? Close the damn blinds!

I shifted around in my chair, adjusted the napkin on my lap, and took another look around the restaurant. It was jammed, not a single table we could move to. Large families with babies and toddlers took up the big tables in the back, where all the shade was. It aggravated the heck out of me. I had to stick it out—focus. I had to overcome it. And while it was the longest brunch of my life, I somehow survived it.

Outside the restaurant (finally, freedom!), I hugged everyone good-bye—George, Terry, Raquel. As I eased into Mom's car, preparing for the hour drive to LAX, the airport just down the road from our apartment, I dismissed the incident that had just occurred in the restaurant as a mystery. "Best left unsolved," I thought, while Mom steered us onto the 405.

Cruising down the same freeway where OJ Simpson once led a nation, I looked forward to my upcoming change of scenery. So long, I said, to the smoggy, gray Southern California horizon. Hello hot and humid Arizona—red, orange, and yellow as far as the eyes can see.

⋯ ⚎✦⚎ ⋯

I've taken hundreds of flights in my life, a result of being shuttled back and forth from LA to Minnesota each summer and winter of my youth. Yet I've never enjoyed planes very much. Maybe it's the turbulence, or that I always flew alone. Or that I felt lost up there at 30,000 feet, torn between two families split so voraciously by divorce.

As a practical-thinking adult, however, I tried to be hopeful and excited about the trip to Arizona.

An hour and a half after reaching the airport, I nestled into a window seat toward the rear of an America West plane—destination: Phoenix Sky Harbor Airport. While I watched a bulky man with headphones down on the tarmac load luggage into the belly of the plane, I noticed my insides had significantly calmed down. I was almost back to normal.

After takeoff, I pulled out the in-flight magazine, opened a bag of salted peanuts, took a sip of my Coke in a small plastic cup, and looked forward to seeing all the green grass of the desert (or at least the burnt orange rocks that cover most driveways out there, including Dad's). Then, as if the daylight coming through all of the windows in the entire plane suddenly went dark, my insides turned upside down.

Whatever blindsided me at the restaurant was back. Now I was really trapped.

Soon, I was attacked by a steady throbbing on the left side of my head—a migraine, the kind I used to get in college, always on one side of the head or the other. Since I had no more of those little yellow pills the doctor at Michigan gave me to counteract them, I tried to wait it out. But the piercing Southern California sun came back, flooding the plane. It made the throbbing worse. I walked to the bathroom in the back of the plane, splashed some water on my face, and took a moment. When I came out, I heard some flight attendants talking in the galley.

"Is there any aspirin back here?" I asked them as I massaged the left side of my head. The pain had gone down the side of my face, giving me a toothache.

One of them told me there were no aspirin on the plane, but the other offered me some from her purse.

"Let me check," she said and then found a small bottle of Tylenol.

"I just need one," I said, squeezing my left eye, which sometimes made the pain in my face go away—a little.

"Here's two," she said. "Hope you feel better."

The flight attendant's kind gesture did make me feel better, but only for a moment. When I got back to my seat, the sky fell again. I started sweating like Ted Striker during the final scene of *Airplane*, when he tries to land the doomed airliner. I placed my head in my hands, turned away from the man sitting next to me, and waited for the storm to pass.

Luckily, it was a short flight to Phoenix, about an hour from LAX. I soon stood outside Sky Harbor in the median of the pickup area, waiting for a shuttle bus to take me to Dad's house. (Dad stopped picking me up from the airport long ago, the Phoenix traffic having become too much for him, he said.)

Since Dad's house is tucked away in one of the many retirement communities in Sun City West, I was always the last person dropped off. As the other riders engaged in pleasant chitchat, no doubt looking forward to their vacations, I rocked back and forth in the last row, the unrelenting Arizona sun accompanying me the whole bumpy, 45-minute drive. By the time I arrived at Dad's, I felt like I'd been put through a popcorn machine—the heat, the shaking, the feeling of sticky butter poured over me. I still don't know how I was able to pay the driver and lug my heavy suitcase to the front door.

After struggling up the driveway, I rang the doorbell, panting like a sick dog.

When the door opened, Dad and Geri were there to greet me. I ducked their open arms and made a beeline for the bathroom. "I'm sick," I said, as I turned the corner into the hallway leading to the guest bedroom. (Later, Geri would tell me my face was so pale, they could tell for themselves something was wrong.)

I stayed in that bedroom—or the bathroom, more accurately—for the next three days, alternating between sweating and shaking on the floor, and puking into the toilet. Geri, an emergency room nurse, finally suggested I go to the hospital where she worked, just up the road. She knew there had to be a problem, especially since I passed on her Christmas dinner the previous night, then declined her and Dad's invitation the following morning to go to Phoenix to see the *Titanic* artifacts exhibit.

I'd already seen the exhibit in Chicago, but that's not why I didn't want to go. I'd have seen it a hundred times if given the chance, just to get another look at the bell that rang from the crow's nest when the iceberg was finally spotted, or one of the lifeboats that bobbed in the freezing water as the *Carpathia* came to the rescue early the following morning, or that two-ton piece of the hull with a pair of portholes still intact—the largest artifact of the ship that's now two and a half miles deep and quickly being eaten away by bacteria. I wanted to see all those things again. If only I could have gotten up off that bathroom floor.

With a wet cloth on my forehead and a plastic bag in my hands, I was driven to the hospital in Geri's Honda. "This is all a waste of time," I assured myself as dusk fell over the empty streets.

As we passed through the sliding glass doors into the emergency room, I noticed the place was mildly busy. I looked at the clock: 5:30 on a Wednesday.

Next thing I knew, I was in a curtain-enclosed examining room, waiting for a doctor to come back with the results of the blood test he'd ordered. Although the test startled me—"Why is he taking my blood?"

I wondered—I was still expecting him to tell me to go home and sleep off this weird flu. "Here, take this," he was supposed to say, handing me a prescription. "Everything will be fine in a couple days."

Dad and Geri sat in the waiting area. I'm sure Geri was fielding a million questions from her coworkers about why she'd come in to work on her day off.

A few minutes later, as I lay on a gurney, using my hand as a pillow—"Why aren't there any pillows here?" I wondered—the doctor returned.

He slipped through the curtains and walked toward me while staring at the clipboard he was holding in his hairy hands. (I could see them clearly at eye level.) A moment later, he raised his eyes, looked at me with an unsympathetic glance, and reported, "We examined your blood"—there was a slight pause, though I didn't know whether my brain had missed a beat or the doctor had taken a breath—"and we think it might be leukemia."

For a second, I had to replay his words in my mind. "Did he actually say that? How is that possible?" I was shocked. "This doctor clearly has no idea what he's talking about. Now he's asking me questions about my medical history. What's the deal? Doesn't this guy know who I am? I'm a reporter! *I'm* the one who asks the questions. I write about *other* people's tragedies. Not my own! And what is his problem anyway, telling me news like this without calling my dad and his own ER nurse in here?"

What upset me even more was that I didn't have anything to say. I'd just been leveled with the most devastating news of my life (even though I still thought it was completely bull) and I didn't have anything to say?

I *always* have something to say. I'm the first one to break a silence, especially when I'm working.

"It's all right," I tell any weary interviewee. "Whatever you can tell me is perfect. Just describe what happened."

Now, with nothing to say, I felt like I had no defense for myself. I viewed each word I should have been speaking as possible ammunition I could fire back at this doctor. And I had nothing!

While I continued to draw a blank, and felt embarrassed for it—he stared at me, waiting for a reaction—I started to recall the bumps I'd been getting on my neck. Lymph nodes! I should have known. And the hemorrhoid I hadn't told anyone about? I knew I'd have to come clean about that too.

Mercifully, the doctor left me alone after saying he was going to order a bone marrow biopsy to verify his findings. As I continued to wait alone in the curtain-enclosed examining room, I started to think about Anders, the Ann Arbor boy with leukemia I had written about two summers earlier. I was blown away that this doctor was actually suggesting my life may have just imitated art. My point? I write a story about a kid with leukemia, and then I get it? Come on! It's ludicrous.

I was confused, angry. I looked around the room, searching for anything sane to wrap my head around. I couldn't. Nothing but sterile hospital equipment.

My return flight to Michigan was in a couple days. I was finally going to shape up, make good on Rod's decision to adopt *me*, a sportswriter of all people, as his friend, his teammate. His ace.

A few minutes later, I was writhing in pain as a large piece of my pelvic bone was yanked out with a long needle. *So this is a bone marrow biopsy.* As I struggled to catch my breath—it felt like the life had just been pulled out of me, the deepest, most penetrating pain I'd ever felt—the doctor said the marrow would be examined to see if his findings were correct, that my blood was diseased.

A half hour later, a wait that felt more like 10 hours, the doctor returned with his clipboard. Dad and Geri were with me by then.

He said he was correct; my blood was not right. I would have to be admitted, more tests would have to be done. Dad and Geri looked at me. I looked at them but didn't say anything. All I was thinking was that I was officially a cancer patient. Again.

<hr />

Once settled into a bed upstairs in the intensive care unit, a nurse placed an IV in my arm. "Just like the good ol' days," I said, as facetious as I'd ever been. I started thinking about my job, and the call I had to make. What would I tell my boss?

Things were getting hazy. It was hard for me to focus. I became angrier at the nurses, the doctors—everybody. Even myself. I thought maybe my pursuit to reach the top of the sportswriting world had worn me down so much, I had driven myself to sickness. All those late nights, the malnutrition, going to sporting events and press conferences on my day off just to land the big story. That's how I got the Woodson scoop—I crashed his charity golf tournament.

When I made the call to my boss the next morning, I was already numb with medication. They'd been shooting me full of chemotherapy and morphine all night long, and a lot of other stuff, I'm sure.

"I'm not coming into work on Monday," I told my boss as I watched the activity in the ICU, the overnight nurses handing off to the refreshed morning crew.

"You better not tell me you're sick, Rom," my boss said. This is the same one who used to call me at the coffee shop, hounding me about my stories. "I have a nasty cold, and I'm taking off most of next week."

"I have you beat," I told him.

"What are you talking about, Rom? I'm busy here. You called right at deadline, and I—"

"I have leukemia."

My boss suddenly got quiet.

"I just found out," I explained. "I'm in a hospital in Arizona, and I don't know how long I'll be here."

My boss apologized. He sounded somber.

"Listen, Rom, whether it takes five days or five years, you'll have your job waiting for you when you get back. Don't even worry about doing any paperwork. We'll take care of it. You just get better. I'll let everyone know what's going on."

I thanked my boss. I was genuinely moved by his support, and that of the paper.

By late morning, I got a call from my mom. Geri handed me the phone. Mom was calm, almost businesslike. She said she was on her way to pick me up.

"I don't remember calling her," I told Geri as I handed her back the phone.

"I spoke with your mom yesterday," she said. "She's made arrangements to take you to the hospital where you were treated for your first cancer. It'll be better for you there; they have more doctors that specialize in the type of leukemia you have. And you'll be closer to home so your mother can take care of you."

After Mom made the six-hour drive to Arizona—first she picked up Nana in Palm Springs, a straight shot down the 10 freeway—she gave a quick hello to Dad and Geri at the curb, helped me from the wheelchair into the car, and got our trip underway. An agonizing drive on the desolate Arizona stretch of the 10 awaited—about 280 miles worth—then an eternity on the LA part of the freeway: a perennial parking lot. I was a wreck by the time we arrived at the hospital's emergency room well after dark, sweating, tired, scared.

I thought at least I might finally get a chance to rest, to get rid of the headache I'd had since Blythe. (It came on right when we passed the WELCOME TO CALIFORNIA sign.) But I had a four-hour stay in the waiting area ahead—with a migraine headache and the sickest amongst us draped in chairs beside me. And with *Jerry Springer* on the television! Of all the shows ever made, *Jerry Springer* for heaven's sake.

"How can they play that garbage in here?" I asked Nana, who just gripped her purse and chewed nervously on her mint gum. Her look of shock mirrored mine.

"They should be playing *I Love Lucy* or *The Sound of Music*—something positive, uplifting."

People around us spoke foreign languages, loudly. Kids were crying. Some were running around. (One nearly bumped into us.) People were walking in and out of a smoking area outside, behind a big glass door. When I smelled the secondhand smoke coming through the bottom of the door, I jumped out of my skin. I couldn't take it anymore.

I got up and slowly walked to the check-in area. There were three tellers, like at a bank. I picked the one in the middle. I sat in a chair in front of the woman's partitioned desk and asked to get a room. She looked at me suspiciously.

"They're expecting me," I told her. "There's a doctor expecting me. I have to get a room."

When she didn't respond (at least not how I wanted, telling me just to wait), I got the doctor's name from Mom and gave it to her.

"Please," I said. "There's actually a doctor expecting me. I have to lie down. I have a migraine headache!"

Eventually, the woman demanded I go sit down. When I didn't, when I stood firm, she threatened to call security.

"Go ahead," I said.

When she did, an officer soon arrived. He stood over me. I could see his gun at eye level.

"If you don't get up, I'm going to arrest you," he said.

If that wasn't hell, I don't know what is.

I stood up and walked into the carbon monoxide–filled garage. I saw the cars, saw Mom's car. It was cold in there. There was a yellowish glow everywhere. It made my headache worse. Physically, I was there. But mentally, I had checked out.

I was gone.

CHAPTER SIXTEEN

Hope Rises

— ⚜ —

> *"We must accept finite disappointment,*
> *but we must never lose infinite hope."*
> —Martin Luther King Jr.

Some time later, I awoke upstairs in the oncology ward. I saw a morphine pump in my hand, an IV pole beside me. Mom and Nana were in the room, sitting in chairs by the window. They were talking, watching TV. Soap operas were on.

"How long have I been here?" I asked. I didn't get an answer. *Did they hear me?*

I was so weak I could barely speak. I wondered whether maybe I hadn't even asked the question, but merely thought it. I felt hungry, tired, like a man stranded in a desert for weeks. I tried to drift back to sleep, but I couldn't stop thinking of how lost I was. Before I closed my eyes, I saw Mom walk over to my bed and whisper something to me, but I didn't hear her.

— ⚜ —

"What's up, bro?"

The booming voice startled me. I opened my eyes: it was Rod, walking into my hospital room. He looked larger than life, like a mountain on legs. He had on his Ravens NFC championship hat. It was turned backward, the way he wore it in Michigan. He dropped his NFL-issue duffel bag on the tiled floor and walked over to my bed. Rod leaned in, I leaned a little toward him, and he gave me a bear hug that nearly crushed me. At first I thought I was dreaming when I opened my eyes and saw him, but my squashed ribs told me otherwise.

I fell back into bed, weak as I'd ever been, and watched Rod scan the room, acclimating himself to his new surroundings. I wondered how could this be. Rod hadn't even told me he was coming. Or had he?

I remembered phoning him before I left the last hospital. I remembered I was angry.

"Don't pick me up from the airport tomorrow," I said.

"Why not?"

"You're not going to believe this . . . I have leukemia."

But everything else about that conversation is a blur. All I remember is that I needed a game plan from Rod, some way to help me cope with my devastating news. I guess he decided to deliver it in person. Maybe that's what Mom was trying to tell me: she and Nana were going to pick Rod up from the airport.

I watched Rod walk over to me again. He took off his hat, leaned against the guardrails on my bed, and played with the machines attached to my IV pole.

"These are nice," Rod said. He was calm, like we were just hanging out at my apartment back home, watching ESPN, talking about everything we talk about.

Suddenly he got serious.

"You ready to knock this out?"

The way Rod asked me, it didn't sound like a question, but rather a statement. An order. I suddenly pictured him before a game, in all of those stadiums across the country, saying the same thing to his teammates.

"You ready to do this?"

They all circle him, jumping up and down. They're ready.

Next, Rod pulled out a flag from his duffel bag—dark blue with a block *M* in the middle. He said Jessica, my girlfriend, gave it to him to bring to me. She had wanted to come out here too, when I told her the news of my illness. I told her to wait: I didn't want her to see me in this vulnerable condition. (I was hardly the picture of confidence she remembered from the sushi restaurant.) Plus, I had wanted to deal with this on my own, like I'd dealt with everything else in my life.

That plan changed. I was glad it had. I didn't think I could handle this one on my own. Leukemia is not like my first cancer. Back then, nobody told me I could have died. Now, I'm well aware of the deadly consequences of my disease.

With Rod beside me, it suddenly felt like the overwhelming weight of this illness—like the problems I had back in Michigan when I first met him—wasn't as heavy anymore. It was as if Rod had lifted the bulk of the weight off of me, just enough to allow me to collect myself and let the haze, as well as the anger that I initially greeted my illness with, clear. I was starting to see straight again, for the first time since Mom and I drove to that San Fernando Valley restaurant.

I was ready to do this.

⊷ ⚊⊪⬩⊪⚊ ⊷

One month later, things are different.

Rod is gone, back to Michigan. Now, at Day 36 in the hospital, I am a shell of myself. I weigh 40 pounds less than when I left Michigan just six weeks ago. Worse, my strength and energy are completely gone. I am in no way prepared to face the risky bone marrow transplant I'll need to survive my illness.

The diseased white blood cells that took over 80 percent of my blood have been reduced to less than five percent—remission. But I am not in the clear yet. I have a chromosome—Philadelphia K positive—that my doctors tell me 70 percent of Americans have. It guarantees the cancer will return, that my remission won't last. Otherwise, I'd be making plans to go back to Michigan right now.

When Mom and I were told my immune system would be zapped to zero during the transplant to accept the donor's blood and that a common cold could kill me in that state, we started searching for other avenues of medical care. The calamities that have occurred in this university research hospital simply can't continue. These doctors—my so-called team—have never treated me like a real teammate. I've been nothing more than a name and a disease on a chart.

It's taken a few days, but Mom and I have found that other avenue: the City of Hope National Medical Center, just nearby here in Pasadena. The City of Hope, we learned from its Web site, is a leader in bone marrow transplants (BMTs). It's been doing them since the 1970s. Thanks to a close friend of Nana's, Mrs. Beverly Kline—she and her husband, Sid, are longtime financial donors to City of Hope—we were able to line up a telephone conversation with Dr. Stephen Forman, the director of hematology there. (I remembered his picture from the Web site.)

I'm going to talk to him today from my hospital room. I look at this conversation as a last-ditch opportunity to sell myself, to prove I'm worthy of living.

"Dr. Forman," I say, sitting up in my bed, pillows propped behind me, "to be honest, I'm a winner. I have goals I want to achieve in life. And all these doctors around me are *losers*. And I think they're going to kill me!" Indeed, an undiagnosed blood clot in my arm nearly did.

"I know you guys are winners. You're the leaders at what you do. If you take me on as part of your team, I guarantee I won't let you down."

I'm practically breathless. I gave all I have—all my tears, all my fight, all my hope. I don't know what's going to come from my plea.

"Steve, don't worry," Dr. Forman says, his voice already putting me at ease. "We're going to get you out of there. I'll have my secretary call you in a half hour. She'll make the arrangements, and we'll see you here soon. Hang in there."

Sure enough, 15 minutes later, we get the call. I look at Mom. For the first time since this insanity began, she's speechless.

Usually Mom is always talking, like when she told my doctors about my blood clot, due to an infected PIC line (a permanent suture where the IV goes into the arm). They didn't believe her, so she demanded an ultrasound be done to verify her findings, which it did. Thank God for Mom and her medical background.

"Say good-bye to our losing *team*," I tell her after we make the plans with Dr. Forman's secretary. "We've been traded . . . from the worst team in the league to the best!"

We check out of the hospital the following day. I insist on walking out—no wheelchair—even though I'm dead tired. Before I leave my room, I retrieve the three-quarter-length leather jacket I wore on the plane to LA. I used to wear this coat everywhere back in Michigan, with Rod, with Jessica, at the sporting events I covered. It was a part of me, part of my identity. I used to get compliments on it. I loved it. When I slip it on now, it feels like it's somebody else's: so big and heavy. I start to cry. The weight of it shows me how far I've fallen, how much of my life I've lost. I quickly pick myself up, however. I want to climb back now. I want to regain my identity

Mom, Nana, and I drive from the hospital directly to the City of Hope's 112-acre campus in Duarte, about an hour northeast of downtown LA. As we approach the entrance to the facility, we're greeted by a giant fountain. It's topped with a bronze sculpture—a man and woman hoisting a baby, the City of Hope's logo.

We find a parking spot nearby and walk to the entrance. I have to lean against Mom. I also hang onto Nana's arm. I'm such a mess it almost makes me laugh. Almost.

"I can get the car and drive you the rest of the way," Mom says.

"No! I *want* to walk. If I didn't, I would have told you to valet the car, so I could've gotten out by the front door. Let's just walk."

Along the way, we notice a botanical garden, with its streams and many bridges. We see elaborate artwork adorning the walkways. One piece, a metal sculpture maybe 12 feet tall, catches my eye. It has a message inscribed in it: THERE IS NO PURPOSE IN CURING THE BODY IF IN THE PROCESS YOU DESTROY THE SOUL. This isn't just any hospital we're going to, I'm starting to believe.

Soon, we're in an examining room, waiting to meet my new doctor. We will have only one doctor, which means I won't have to constantly repeat myself like I did at the other hospital. We always got so frustrated when my team members kept stumbling into my room one after the other during the course of the day. *Hi, how are you feeling?* Half-hour later: *Hi, how are you feeling?*

"Didn't you talk to the other guy?" I'd say.

"They don't communicate with each other," Mom would tell me. "It's like one hand doesn't wash the other."

Even though it was a short walk from the parking lot, I'm exhausted as we wait for the doctor. I'm hunched over in a chair in the corner of the examining room, Nana sitting beside me, Mom standing next to her. I'm happy to be here, happy to be out of that other hospital, but I'm still worried that every doctor in this field is just as bad as the ones I've dealt with the past month.

Before long, Dr. David Snyder walks in. He's holding my phonebook-thick medical chart, staring at it intently. "Here we go again," I'm thinking, "just a number and a disease on a chart."

"It says here you're a sportswriter," Dr. Snyder says, looking up at me with inquisitive eyes.

Where is this going? He's not talking about my disease. He's not talking about my chances of survival, which I was told at the other hospital is between 40 and 70 percent.

"Yeah. So what?"

"Well," Dr. Snyder says, "I'm from Boston. I'm a big fan of the Red Sox, and the Patriots, of course. I see the Celtics play whenever they're in town. They're doing very well this year."

He's talking sports? I can't believe it.

I remember watching a college basketball game shortly after I checked into the last hospital. When my doctors came into the room during one of their first consultations, they all filed in and stood in front of the TV. I was alone at the time. Normally I don't get into college hoops until March and the NCAA Tournament, but for whatever reason I was really into this game. It was the first real reprieve I'd had since I learned of my disease. It provided me a small porthole to happier times. And my doctors just stood in front of the TV, slamming that porthole shut. They rattled off treatments and numbers to each other, not even looking at me. I waited for one of them to notice I was watching the game and ask, "Who's playing?" or "What's the score?" But there was nothing.

"Did you see the Super Bowl?" Dr. Snyder asks me, referring to the New England Patriots' win over the highly favored St. Louis Rams a couple days earlier.

"I did," I say. "I liked how the Patriots were introduced as a team instead of individually before the game. My friend Rod played for the Ravens when they won the Super Bowl last year. He said the Patriots won that game before it even started because of that display of solidarity."

"Oh, fantastic," Dr. Snyder says, nodding his head in accordance.

Dr. Snyder has a soft, mellow voice, it can put you to sleep if you're not careful. It calms me.

Our sports discussion goes on a few more minutes. And as Dr. Snyder and I talk, I no longer feel like a cancer patient, because I'm talking about, and thinking about, something I love.

"By the way," Dr. Snyder says, looking down at my chart. "It looks like you'll need to have a bone marrow transplant."

Suddenly, I'm worried. Back to a name and number on a chart, I'm thinking. I look at Mom and Nana. The smiles they've had since Dr. Snyder walked into the room are gone. They look like they're in the front seat of a roller coaster just before the big fall.

"Well," Dr. Snyder says, "we'll find you a donor, you'll have your transplant, and you'll be back to work in no time."

There will be no fall, it appears. In fact, it feels like Dr. Snyder has just put me on his back. It's like he's saying, "Hang on, Steve. I'll carry you to victory. Let's just ride it out." And while I'm still hunched over in a chair, still drooling into a Styrofoam cup I carry everywhere because my saliva production has gone haywire—it's either this or swallow a mouthful of drool, which will make me sick—I feel better than I have in weeks.

As we drive home, I tell Mom and Nana that Dr. Snyder reminds me of a coach who comes into the locker room at halftime after his players were just beaten down in the first half. "Hey!" he says, slamming the door behind him. "Pick your heads up! I don't care what happened out there. We're still going to win this game. We're going to do exactly what we worked on in practice. We're going to unite as a team. And we're going to go out there and *earn* this victory. Period! And I don't care *who* the opponent is!"

"If Rod is my team captain," I tell Mom and Nana, "I think we've just found our head coach in Dr. Snyder."

During the wait for the transplant, I spend most of my days driving with Mom to the City of Hope for outpatient treatments. (Nana has returned to Palm Springs.) I need blood transfusions twice a week, along with the occasional platelet transfusion. I don't know what platelets are, but Mom becomes frantic when Dr. Snyder informs us that my counts are low in that department. She tells me to stay put, then rushes to a clinic clear across campus to donate hers for me. A short time later, Mom sits by my side the entire three-plus hours it takes for them to disappear into my veins. Mom, in fact, recently gave her blood to see if she can be a donor for my transplant, but no luck. Still, it was amazing to think her blood, the same blood that first gave me life, could have possibly saved it.

Rod, for his part, also gave blood to see if he could be a donor for me. He participated in a blood drive along with more than 90 of my coworkers. They actually had a team from the Red Cross come to the newsroom one day. While no one was a match for me, they're all in the bone marrow registry now, and can possibly help someone else someday.

All of my transfusions take three to four hours, either the blood; platelets; or TPN (therapeutic nutrients and vitamins), which will help me gain some weight back. That's three to four hours of sitting in a plastic-covered recliner in a room crowded with patients. Some of them sleep while the IV does its job. Others watch daytime talk shows on the ceiling-mounted TV. Still others jabber away on their cell phones, making business deals or gossiping with friends or family members, like everything is normal. Those are the good patients, the tolerable ones.

Some, if you make eye contact with them, stare at you. Or maybe you get lucky and they're too busy talking on the phone or to their caregiver to even notice you. Other patients cry, moan, or get sick, either in a small plastic bin a nurse gives them, or if that's not handy, all over themselves. As I sit in my recliner during all of this, watching that same beet-red blood flow into my veins, I find it hard to comprehend what's happening. "Do I look like them?" I wonder. I don't want to look like them.

"What in the hell are we doing here?" I ask Mom, usually after someone throws up. She just shakes her head. "God forbid," she says.

— ◆ —

Every outpatient visit starts with a blood test. A nurse, usually a short Spanish lady, takes between five and 10 vials from my left arm, just below my bicep. (This is where I ask for it; there's a good vein there, fat). Then the lab tests my white counts, red counts, and every other count I can think of to make sure the leukemia is still in remission. Meanwhile, the City of Hope searches for a donor.

Who knows how long it will take to find one. It took three weeks just to finish the insurance paperwork to get the search started. I'm sure it would have taken longer had Dr. Snyder not been the assistant director of oncology here.

You don't want to disappoint Dr. Snyder, I'm guessing. He gives speeches about his work all over the country. And he's a leader in the creation of a new miracle drug, Gleevec. It's designed to keep leukemia at bay for years, maybe forever, should the patient never find a bone marrow transplant donor. Gleevec, I'm told by the pharmacist when we take home a sample, is $3,000 a bottle—100 pills. I do the math: that's $30 a pill, or should I live to be 85 and take the required one a day, $602,250.

If I had a choice, I'd want the transplant: one and done; I could get on with my life. But again, it might take weeks, months, even years for the donor squad to locate one for me, even with my doctor's prestige.

I'm told my blood has to match at six HLA antigen levels (proteins on the surface of the cell that helps the immune system distinguish the body's own cell from other people's), so it's not just the blood type that needs to line up like I had thought. If we do find a six-of-six match (even a four-of-six if we're desperate), it has to then align at 24 molecular levels, Mom tells me. I don't like those odds. Also, the donor must be under age 65, even though he or she could have donated blood to the National Marrow Donor Program decades ago.

Assuming a match is found for me through the bone marrow registry, which is part of a worldwide donor database of over six million, the person still has to be contacted. So that person will have to reside at the same address as when the sample was given, or will need to have notified the program otherwise. (Sure, an Internet search can be done, but there are no guarantees.) And, most important, the donor has to be healthy, not struggling with his or her own medical problems. The way things are today, with one in every 20 Americans diagnosed with some type of cancer each year, even that can be a toss-up. The planets, the stars—heck, the whole universe—will have to align for me to make it through this.

Remarkably, I maintain a steady calm within this universe of uncertainty. I credit this to Dr. Snyder, who is doing everything he can to get me back to work, back to Michigan, like he said. I'm also bolstered by thinking about the progress I've made since I left LA, and how much I now have to live for.

I have plans, goals, many of them with Rod. I often think about him, along with the rest of my life in Michigan. When I do, I think about all the good times Rod and I had, as well as all the stories he told me about his years in Ann Arbor. I'm reminded of those stories now, as

I while away the hours in this plastic-covered recliner. One involved a game against the University of Wisconsin, on the road in Madison.

"I was running down a Wisconsin defender, trying to lay down a block for my running back," Rod said. "I caught up with the guy right near the Wisconsin sideline—and drilled him! Completely laid him out. Thing is, I hit the guy so hard, we both went down. Knocked out!"

"What happened?" I asked. "Did you go out of the game?"

"No way. I remember finally coming to and hearing my teammates cheering for me from across the field. They were yelling, 'Way to go, Rod! Great hit! Great hit, Rod!' Do you know the only reason I wanted to get up before that other guy was because of them? That was the only thing."

When Rod told me that story, I couldn't believe how he summoned that kind of strength, that kind of will, just by hearing some faint cheers from across the field. But now I can. I can hear my own cheers now, from everyone who reached out to me during the beginning stages of my illness.

As I continue to watch the blood pour into me during this endless series of transfusions, I can hear all those people who sent me cards and letters and phoned me (even if I was too sick to talk) when I first checked into the hospital. They're my family members, coworkers, friends, friends of friends, many of whom I didn't even know— strangers. They all cheered for me, both near and far, and are still cheering. I consider them my teammates—Team Rom—and if I go down, they all do. I'm not going to let that happen.

As for my biggest teammate, my team captain, what Rod did for me during those beginning stages of my battle was truly unforgettable: MVP-type stuff. Because of his unselfishness, I was able to have a teammate pull me up from the turf after I collided with this potentially deadly opponent.

I was sure to tell Rod this during the last night of his four-day stay in the hospital six weeks ago. He needed to get back to his radio job, he said, otherwise he would have stayed longer. At any rate, he would only be a phone call away. After Rod cleared the room of my family

members and hospital personnel again—using a softer tone this time—
I propped myself up, sitting as high as possible in the bed.

"I don't care if I ever make it out of here," I told him. "I'm serious.
I'm just happy to know I finally have what I always wanted in life—a
brother, someone who will always be there for me. And here you are.
That's all I needed. . . . I've already made it out of here. I've already
won."

Rod and I hugged, we prayed, we cried. We vowed we'd see each
other again, even though it was a promise we didn't know whether we
could keep.

Thinking about Rod's stay in the hospital puts me at ease during
my transfusion, because I know I will finally be able to keep that
promise I made to him before he left. And Rod is on a plane headed for
LA, his second visit to help rally me back to health.

CHAPTER SEVENTEEN

This Is Recovery

*"I learned that if you want to make it bad enough,
no matter how bad it is, you can make it."*
—GALE SAYERS

od is coming to LA with friends who will rent a car at the airport and drop him off at my apartment, then visit some of their family members nearby. As the hour approaches midnight this first Friday in February 2002, I start to lose some of the excitement I had the previous few days in anticipation of Rod's arrival. I'm just too tired to be excited. Usually, I'm asleep well before the ten o'clock news. So when the doorbell rings at 11:43, I have to drag myself up from the couch I drifted away on.

I open the door and see Rod standing in the brightly lit hallway, where I used to hide my house key underneath the fire hydrant. As Rod walks in, I'm expecting a bear hug, like I got in the hospital. Instead, he just walks past me.

"You look like you just got out of a concentration camp," he says as he takes a seat on the couch I just got up from. And although I'm stunned by what Rod has said, I'm not really surprised. Rod is being Rod, saying what's on his mind, even if it hurts.

Thing is, he's right. As I close the door, I realize this is the first time I've thought about how bad I look since I checked out of the hospital. I'm all of 135 pounds, not a hair on my head, and practically drowning in the red sweatshirt and sweatpants that fit me like an Isotoner glove only a month earlier.

I take a seat on the flower-patterned chair that matches the couch and, for the next few minutes, Rod and I sit in the living room zoning out. We hardly talk.

"How was the flight?" I ask him.

"All right," he says, offering nothing else. Instead of talking, we watch David Letterman on the small TV in the kitchen, the one with the antenna that's been broken since CBS's Friday-night lineup included *Dukes of Hazzard* and *Dallas*. The picture is a little snowy, but we can still see it.

Thinking of the thousands of meals Mom and I had in that kitchen—and the thousands of TV programs we watched there—I start to comprehend the magnitude of this moment: Rod, sitting here in this apartment, where I made all those personal transformations over the years. It makes me wonder exactly who I am now.

I haven't thought about it much, even though I've had all the time in the world the past month and a half to do it. Right now, I feel torn between the life I forged back in Michigan and the one that's still here. I'm simply not able to shake free of this city, this apartment. It's difficult to think about this, almost too much to handle during this ongoing time of uncertainty. The tension in the room isn't helping much either. Thankfully, Rod soon breaks the silence. It feels like a grizzly bear has jumped off my back.

He tells me what's been happening back home, what he's been up to.

"Not much of anything," he says, "just hanging out at the car shop, working out at the Building." I start to think Rod may have finally gotten over the shock of my appearance. He seems a little more relaxed.

Rod quickly gets to the reason for his second trip to LA.

"You need to recover *physically* to get ready for that transplant," he says. "Look at you. You've got a long way to go. That's what caught me off-guard when I saw you. I was like, 'Damn!'"

I can understand that. I haven't done much to help myself since I left the hospital. I haven't swallowed a solid bite. Instead, I've been drinking Gatorade and some canned protein drinks that taste awful (even the chocolate-flavored ones). My throat doesn't burn anymore, but I haven't eaten in so long. I guess I've lost the will. Plus, my taste buds are still shot. Everything has a horrible copper taste, like I'm sucking on a penny.

I explain this to Rod, but he just hops to his feet like he did in the hospital when I was having my temper tantrum, and heads to the kitchen.

"Don't worry, bro," he says. "It's hard to eat, but I've been there. You can do it."

I follow Rod to the kitchen, where he opens the large pantry cupboard. It's filled with canned food, cereal boxes, crackers, old paper plates and Styrofoam cups. Most of it was around when I left for college. Rod reaches in and pulls out a can of beef stew.

As I watch Letterman from the kitchen table, Rod empties the stew into a small pot and places it on the stove. He goes to the refrigerator and pulls open the crisper drawer. He finds a sealed package of cheddar and jack cheese squares.

While Rod stirs the pot of stew with a long wooden spoon, I watch New England Patriots kicker, Adam Vinatieri, boot a football off the roof of the Ed Sullivan Theater in New York City, where Letterman is filmed.

I remember watching Vinatieri kick the game-winning field goal in the Super Bowl about a week ago. This kick sails toward the waiting arms of Donald Trump, who's standing in a parking lot atop a building a block away from the Ed Sullivan. He drops it. Actually, the Don doesn't even come close to catching it. Rod and I both laugh.

"Outrageous," Rod says as he continues to stir the pot.

"Did you ever do anything that cool following the Super Bowl last year?" I ask Rod.

"Not really," he says, tasting the stew.

When Letterman goes to commercial, Rod dishes the stew into a soup bowl. He opens the bag of cheese cubes, tosses a few into the bowl, and places the colorful creation in front of me.

"This is for me?" I quip. I thought it was for Rod. He knows I can't eat.

"Dang right it's for you," he says, standing over me.

The stew does look tasty, but I can't get myself to taste it. I've tried to eat. Mom, for her part, has pressed me to eat since I've been home. But as I've continually told her, I can't. She's respected that.

Why doesn't Rod?

"I appreciate you making this," I tell him, picking at the stew with my fork, spreading the steam around. "But it just hurts too much to eat."

"Just try it," he says.

I look at the bowl, so daunting.

"It hurts," I say.

Rod says nothing more. He just turns around, opens the silverware drawer and rummages through it.

A second later, he slaps a tablespoon in front of me.

"Eat, dammit!" he says, snatching the fork out of my hand. "This is recovery now!"

"I can't!" I say, as loud as I can, but it's only a whisper next to Rod's bellow.

Rod grabs the spoon off the table and jams it in the stew.

"I don't care if it hurts," he says. "You think I wanted to eat after all those surgeries? You *have* to eat now. This is survival!"

After chewing on those words, I scoop up a spoonful and, as much as it pains me, eat it. Then I force down another spoonful. And another. By the last one, I am on my way to recovery.

I will need to get there. I will need to gain back some of the weight I lost for the risky bone marrow transplant. I will be extremely vulnerable with my immune system so weak. That's the part I remember most about the procedure—a common cold can kill me! I will be at the mercy of everyone: doctors, nurses, other patients, my family and friends. Once again, like when I wiggled my fingers and toes before those spinal taps, I'll feel completely powerless.

"Remember what I told you in the hospital," Rod says, after I share my concern about the transplant. "No matter what you do, God is always in control. I'll be there to help you, along with those doctors and nurses, but *he*'s ultimately going to take care of you. You still need to get your strength up, though. So keep eating, keep training. Don't worry, I'll help you."

As I put the bowl into the sink—I manage to eat about half of the stew—Rod goes over more ways I can get into shape.

Clean up around the house, he tells me. Throw out some of the old stuff in the cupboard, as well as the junk that has accumulated all over the apartment since I left for college (and the decades prior to that). "You'll need a clean environment," Rod insists. "Or you can't get to where you want to be."

The next morning, we have breakfast at Dinah's, the same restaurant at which I celebrated my junior high school graduation. While I want to order my usual giant apple-cinnamon pancake, my lack of taste buds forces me to stick with oatmeal. After we order, Rod briefs Mom on the game plan to get me back in shape.

"He's going to need a clean environment to do this," Rod says.

"I know. His immune system is already weak," Mom responds.

"Have you seen that apartment? He can't live there. Something has to be done."

"I know, I know," Mom pleads.

"That's not enough!" Rod leans over the table so he doesn't have to yell. People at the next table are looking at us. "That apartment should have been clean before he got home."

Rod's right, but I know Mom didn't have the time. She woke up at three in the morning every day to work a few hours at the office before driving to the hospital to be there when I got up. I don't know what I would have done if she hadn't been around to keep tabs on those doctors.

"That was more important at the time than a clean apartment," I tell Rod.

"I understand that," he says. "If you need to hire a maid to help, go ahead and do it. But you *need* to clean up that apartment." He's looking at Mom. "You can start by throwing out a lot of the stuff that's collecting dust on those shelves in the living room."

When Mom still balks at the idea—she actually sheds a tear at the thought of throwing out a lot of her old trinkets, mostly kitchenware that hasn't been used since she received them as wedding gifts—Rod gives her the "recovery" talk. Then he says he'll give us the money to hire a maid, if financial issues are the problem.

"Things are *that* bad," he says. "You need to throw out a lot of that stuff."

When Mom continues to resist, Rod tells her I might have to go stay with Nana at her condominium in Palm Springs until the transplant. In fact, we're heading there later today, to relax (and take the edge off, hopefully). I had told Rod about Nana's place, how nice and spacious it is there—and extremely tidy. I didn't think it registered with him, but he remembered, apparently.

"I *will* help clean up," Mom says, "but I can't throw away those things. They're family heirlooms."

Mom starts to calm down and begins eating her omelet. While Rod gulps down his hash browns, eggs, and blueberry pancakes, I think about what he's just said.

He would actually give *us* the last of his NFL money? This is the stash that's been depleted by the house he bought in Cincinnati (now long gone), as well as the funds needed to take care of his mom and all those compounding medical bills of his. What a friend.

When we get home, Rod starts digging through the countless boxes of photographs I still have sitting around my bedroom.

"When did you get this," he says, holding a picture of me leaning against my first car—a red Chevy Camaro with limo tint on all the windows.

"I bought it at the end of my senior year in high school. Actually, my family pitched in to help. There were only nine miles on the speedometer. Suddenly, I became a lot more popular at Uni."

"Uni?"

"University High. It's in Santa Monica."

"What was it like?"

"It was pretty cool. There wasn't a lot of morale at the school; no one really supported the teams. But we did have a lot of celebrities go there."

"Like who?"

"I actually sat next to the older brother in *The Wonder Years* during health class my first year—Jason Hervey. He was also in *Back to the Future*: the kid at the dinner table who, when the family was watching TV, asked, 'What's a rerun?' I also knew a dude who ended up on *Baywatch*. I didn't really know him, but I saw him around a lot."

Rod continues to study the 16-inch, cast aluminum wheels and black bra I had on my Camaro. (Rod is a big car enthusiast. He wants me to buy a vintage Corvette, one of my dream cars, so he can restore it like new.) He soon finds other slices of my life captured on film: my skydiving trip in Hemet, near Palm Springs; my trips to Alaska and Hawaii in junior high, compliments of Nana and a teen-tour company based out of New York; and my many adventures to World Wrestling Federation events as a teenager, where my friends and I used to sneak up to the ringside seats and snap pictures.

"JYD!" Rod says, holding up a picture I took of Junkyard Dog at the Los Angeles Sports Arena. "I loved him. He'd come into the ring with a dog collar and chain around his neck. If I had been a wrestler, I'd have been just like him."

"Just like him?"

"Better. What's up with these guys?" Rod asks, holding a picture of the tattooed millionaire wannabes I played with in my rock bands. "Where are these guys now?"

"One of them, Ritchie B., a drummer from my first band, I saw walking on Hollywood Boulevard about two years ago. He was wearing his trademark cowboy hat and boots (circa 1988 Guns N' Roses). This was long after I quit playing music. I was in LA for my 10-year high school reunion."

"I think my reunion is coming up," Rod says. "I should go."

"You should. It's a kick. Do you know I graduated from Michigan less than a week before my reunion? Just under the gun. Everyone there was in a third career, second marriage. They asked me what I'd been up to since college. I said, 'I went to the mall, saw a movie, then flew out here.'"

As Rod flips through more pictures, I start to drift off. I'm awakened, soon after, by the grumbling of Rod's stomach.

"Where's a good place to eat?" he says, the breakfast we had just an hour ago hardly satisfying him.

"We could go to Jerry's Deli," I tell him, recalling that's where he and Mom went during his first visit to LA, when they ducked out of the hospital and left me with that beeping IV machine.

"Nah. What are some of the hot spots around here? Someplace where we can hang out too." Rod packs up the boxes of photos and pushes them into the closet.

"Well, it is Saturday. The beach is always jumping. We could go to Venice."

Soon, Rod and I are walking along the same boardwalk Jim Morrison once prowled before forming The Doors. I used to go to Venice at least once a week while growing up, either with Mom or friends. We'd watch the famous chainsaw juggler, the skateboarders who make the beach their second home, and the guy with the turban that roller-skates along the sidewalk while playing a white electric guitar with a red target on it. Years later, during college, I saw him in a Janet Jackson music video. "That's the dude from Venice Beach," I told my fraternity brothers as we watched TV in the frat house.

The turban-topped guitar player skates by us, playing the same distorted sounds out of the mini Marshall amplifier strapped to his belt, and I point him out to Rod. Rod seems too wrapped up in the overall beachside ambiance to notice, however. With his shirt off and whipped around his shoulder, and dark glasses on, Rod looks right at home.

"Why don't you take off your shirt, bro?" Rod asks as we walk alongside a stream of bikini-clad girls and camera-wielding tourists. One guy walking toward us has a white-and-yellow boa constrictor around his neck—Albinos, I think they're called.

"I can't," I say, watching the people give extra room to the guy with the snake. "I'm too skinny." Indeed, I might fly off to San Diego or China if a strong wind comes along and catches me off guard. "And my skin's too sensitive," I add, reminding Rod that I've been indoors for more than a month. "Doctors told me to stay out of the sun. I really shouldn't even be out here."

"Just do it," Rod says, raising his arms to his side, puffing out his chest. "We're at the beach. This is LA."

While there's no novelty in that for me, I don't want to disappoint Rod. He seems too happy. I strip my shirt off and whip it over my shoulder, just like he did, and we continue strutting along the boardwalk. While I'm proud to be standing tall out here in the sun with all the healthy, beautiful people (along with all the freaks of nature that make this place so interesting), I still feel extremely self-conscious.

I am so skinny it's embarrassing. At one point, while Rod works out at Muscle Beach, the spot future "Governator" Arnold Schwarzenegger once made so famous—it's right on the boardwalk, in plain view of everyone—I select a puka shell necklace off a storefront rack nearby. I try it on. It's supposed to fit tight, like a choker, but it wears like an 18-inch chain on me. I buy it anyway, for one reason: the day this thing fits me, I will be back to where I want to be.

When I get home, I put the necklace in the box I made in my eighth-grade wood shop class, where I used to keep all my WWF and concert tickets so I wouldn't lose them. Rod and I are both tired from our long afternoon in the hot sun. We decide to take a quick nap before the drive to Palm Springs—him in my room, me on the couch.

After our trip to PS—Nana had fresh chicken salad with sliced celery and capers, and shrimp cocktail on ice waiting for us, which Rod loved—I get more instruction on how to get back in shape.

"Take walks around the block," Rod says, "and keep cleaning up around the house. Throw out as much as you can."

"I will, I will."

After the pep talk, Rod retreats to my bedroom. I assume he wants to get more laughs at the snapshots of life.

"Dude, this ain't you," he says as I walk into the room. "With the long hair and leather chaps?" He's holding a picture of me on stage, when my hair was the longest it's ever been—halfway down my back.

"Yes it is," I say, proudly. Rod still doesn't believe me, so I pop in a video of the same show at which the picture was taken: Slam Alley, live at the Whisky A Go-Go on Sunset Boulevard.

"Slam Alley was one of the more popular bands I played with," I tell Rod, "mostly because the guys in the band really did look like rock stars, tattoos all the way down their arms: 'sleeves,' they're called."

I point out the bass player on the right side of the screen. "That's me."

"Noooo," Rod says, "that dude jumping around all over the place?"

I direct his attention to the lone tattoo on the bass player's left shoulder, a black rose with barbwire wrapped around the stem, then pull up my left shirtsleeve, exposing my scrawny shoulder.

"See," I say. "Same tattoo, only less muscle. My bandmates used to make fun of me for having just one."

Rod laughs—one of his typical bellowing howls.

"That is you! You're jamming up there."

It's funny, while I've never seen Rod play football, he's now seen me play the same stage on which The Doors, Van Halen, and Ratt all started out. Suddenly, my accomplishments don't seem so inconsequential next to his. Well, at least the gap has been bridged a little.

＋・ ☰✦☰ ・＋

Soon, Rod's second four-day visit to help rally me back to health is over. The night of his departure, he and I sit outside my apartment on the steps, waiting for his friends to pick him up. It's a cool night in LA, and Rod and I go over the game plan again. I will have to get stronger for the transplant, Rod says, should God bless me with a donor. We pray for that to happen.

This is a new thing for me—praying, putting the onus of my problems on a higher being instead of trying to fix them myself.

"You know how far that got you," Rod says about relying only on myself in life, never letting anyone break through my protective wall.

"Yeah I do," I say. "I know too well."

"You're going to have to have faith, bro."

We sit silently a few more minutes, watching the cars occasionally motor past us.

"I'm glad we had this chance to sit out here," Rod says. "We've talked about what's important to do. Now it's up to you, bro. You know what has to be done." I nod my head as I look up and down the street for Rod's friends. It's late, about 9:30 on a Monday night. "This is where the rubber meets the road," Rod says, one of his favorite sayings.

Rod's friends soon pull up to the curb in front of the apartment. One gets out and greets us—Niki, a girl I met a few times back in Michigan. She's a longtime friend of Rod's. After catching up with her for a moment, Rod and I say good-bye. We assure each other we'll meet up again soon. As Rod gets into the car, I sit back on the steps— gingerly. I've lost so much weight, I can feel my bones on the concrete.

As the car heads up the hill—the same one my friends and I walked up each day to get to elementary school—I can see the taillights getting smaller in the distance. When the tiny lights finally disappear over the hill, I begin to think it was no coincidence I met Rod when I did, or that he wore wings on his Michigan football helmet all those years.

"There goes an angel," I say, tears welling as I think of everything Rod's done for me since we met. "There goes a true angel."

CHAPTER EIGHTEEN

What's Your Story?

⁘

*"We must use time wisely and forever realize
that the time is always ripe to do right."*
—NELSON MANDELA

The next day, after Mom goes to work, I start gathering things to throw out. I begin with a collection of old vases, many of which are so dirty their glass isn't opaque anymore. Next, I stack the decades worth of magazines that Mom has collected, including *Men's Health*, *Fitness Journal*, and *Cooking Light*, the latter neither of us has ever read. Then I collect the giant cylindrical candles friends have given Mom over the years, some of which haven't been used in so long the wicks have disintegrated. I pack them all generously into grocery bags I find crumpled up in the bottom shelf of the pantry.

In between trips to the trash bins behind the apartment, I sift through the countless artifacts in my room, organizing and throwing out when necessary. With the bags of clothes, kitchenware, and other items Mom and I set aside for Goodwill, and the many bags of junk I throw out, we accumulate about 10 bags a day—50 so far.

Each morning I focus on a new area of the apartment that needs a major overhaul. At night, I call Rod to update him on my progress.

"You should see this place," I say. "You'd hardly recognize it."

This long-overdue spring cleaning really does make a dent in the apartment's disarray. It also gives me a proud feeling—like I'm accomplishing something. As the number of trash bags starts to dwindle to just two or three a day, I find time to return to my writing. This is a huge accomplishment, as even sitting in front of the computer for any amount of time is tiresome. (Having no cushion down there really does present a problem.)

Dr. Snyder, it turns out, has a neighbor who writes for the *Los Angeles Times*. I'd applied at the paper a few years ago only to have its employment recruiter tell me to call back in five years when I had more experience.

"Do you know Larry Stewart?" Dr. Snyder asked me during one of my first outpatient visits.

"I know that name," I said. "Doesn't he do the TV and radio notes for the *Times*."

"Yes, and I thought I could have him come down here and meet you if you'd like."

"Really? That'd be great."

I assumed Dr. Snyder meant when I'm better.

"OK, I'll have him come down during your next appointment."

Two days later, instead of Dr. Snyder walking into my examining room, Larry Stewart came in.

"So I hear you're from Michigan," he said, shaking my hand as I sat on the edge of the table Dr. Snyder usually examined me on. After talking with me about Michigan, the journalism business, and some of the Michigan football games he'd covered—including the 1998 Rose Bowl, when the Wolverines won a share of the national championship with Nebraska—Larry asked if I wanted to do some book reviews for the *Times'* sports section.

"Are you kidding?" I said, jumping out of my oversized clothes. "I can actually write for the *Los Angeles Times*?"

"I'll have to get it approved by our sports editor, Bill Dwyre," Larry said. "But I think it will be all right."

"It's funny," I tell Mom on the way home. "I would have sold my soul to write for the *LA Times* when I was in Michigan. And now I get to do it after I get sick with leukemia?"

"It's truly a wonder how things work out," Mom says.

My book reviews run on Page 2 of the sports section, in its daily "Hot Corner" piece. A Consumer's Guide to the Best and Worst of Sports Media and Merchandise, it states atop each story. I also submit previews of upcoming sports television programs.

I do the stories for free, but I can't put a price on what they mean to me. Seeing my byline in the *Los Angeles Times* truly is a dream come true.

The writing benefits me in other ways. It takes my mind off the wait for a donor, as well as my lingering fatigue. It also gives me an opportunity to see a side of Rod I've never seen before. This, however, is purely by coincidence.

After watching one of Fox Sports Net's "Behind the Glory" preview tapes Larry sent me from the *Times*' downtown building—he gets them a couple weeks before the show airs—I eject the tape and notice the channel is set to ESPN Classic. And as I reach for the remote control to shut off the TV, I see Michigan is playing in the game replay. It's a game against Texas A&M, from the Alamo Bowl. I can see the logo on the field.

Rod played in that game, his junior year. I remember the team photo he once showed me. It had the same 1995 Alamo Bowl logo beneath it.

I instantly recognize Rod's No. 52. He runs onto the field with the rest of the Wolverines' offensive players. A few seconds later, when Rod snaps off the first-down play, I see for the first time—with my own eyes, that is—the type of player he was.

Sure enough, Rod runs down the field as the play unfolds. He's all over the place, blocking for his running back, getting in position to make a tackle in case of a turnover—a "sudden change," he calls it. "That's the mind-set of a team after a fumble or interception," he says.

"You have to react immediately. Especially the defense, because they're the first on the field to clean up the mess." Rod is in the fray, the front lines, like he always told me.

I sit down Indian style in front of the TV, paying close attention to Rod on each play. One after the other, he's in the middle of the action, devoting everything he's got to the game. It looks like he's exhausted after each play, but he just walks back to the line of scrimmage and does it all over again. I remember he once told me playing center is like running full-bore into the base of a tree 60 or 70 times during a three-hour span. "How do you think that feels?" he asked. "I can't even imagine," I told him.

Eventually my legs fall asleep. I get up and scramble to find a VHS tape to record the rest of the game. I locate an old Maxell six-hour—*Rocky III* and *Caddyshack* are on the label. I stick it in the VCR. I decide to forget the movies; I can always buy those. I don't want to miss the end of this game.

Later, I call Rod to tell him what I watched today.

"I saw you on TV. ESPN Classic was showing the Alamo Bowl."

"Oh yeah?" Rod says, his voice lacking enthusiasm.

For Rod, maybe this news isn't such a big deal. But for me it is. Seeing Rod on TV, watching him represent his team and illustrate everything he's told me since we met, gives me a satisfying feeling. He really did give the extra effort like he's always said. And with the pride I now have seeing my childhood apartment slowly improve with each bag of junk I throw out, I start to feel all is not lost. I'm making progress, moving closer to the goal, like a football team marching down the field.

I always remember my dad telling me that football was his favorite sport. "You can be born to play baseball, but you have to *work* at being a football player," he'd say. Sadly, I can't even call him to share what I saw on ESPN Classic. Whenever we talk now, Dad never wants to hear about Rod. He just says hello, asks me how I'm feeling, and passes the phone on to Geri. "Give her the report," he says.

⊷ ⊱✠⊰ ⊷

Despite my frustrations with Dad, I maintain a feeling of hope and accomplishment for a good many days after I saw Rod play on TV. But after a few more rounds of transfusions, I inevitably fall back into one of my funks. They're similar to those that plagued my final months in Michigan.

Indeed, the thrill I had watching Rod earn his future MVP status in the Alamo Bowl just a couple weeks ago is but a distant memory. I feel nervous, anxious, sometimes panicked here in LA. My nerves usually attack me late at night, when I listen to the radio and stare at my bedroom ceiling. I think about Michigan and what remains of my life back there. I know it's the indefinite nature of my situation that's causing this. I like to have an idea of when things are going to happen, as well as how long they'll last. That way I can be in control. I used to always be in control.

When this worry takes over, I try to remember the lessons Rod taught me about overcoming adversity—or, at the very least, remaining calm in the face of turmoil.

"It's mind over matter," Rod used to say. "If you don't mind, it don't matter." It was easy to pull off back home, and thinking of it reminds me of the time Rod and I went to a Michigan field hockey game in a driving rain to watch our friend, Ashley Reichenbach, coach the Wolverines. Thanks to Rod's mantra, we enjoyed the match as if the players were competing under a cloudless sky. It was actually fun, like when I was a kid and ran through sprinklers and didn't care if I got wet. But now it's different—it *does* matter now. And it feels like more than just rain is coming down on me with this disease still infesting my body.

This tense feeling I have is similar to an episode that occurred at the university research hospital, just after Rod went back to Michigan. It began when a chemotherapy treatment—an important one—was delayed more than an hour, and I was having trouble breathing.

Again, I like to know when my treatments will take place. That way I can mentally prepare for them, psych myself up, which is how I got through all those spinal taps.

I recall that episode now, as I stare at the ceiling in my old bedroom. I keep replaying it in my mind to see how I was able to locate a calm and get over it. I was pressing the nurse call button, but getting no response. I wanted to know what the delay was.

My breaths were getting heavy. Soon, I was hyperventilating.

"You're having a panic attack," Mom said.

I was gasping like the air conditioner in my apartment in Michigan. I was nearly choking. I had no choice: I had to send the Bat-Signal.

"Call Rod," I told Mom.

Mom dialed Rod's cell phone and handed me hers.

"What'd you do when this happened to a freshman before a big game?" I asked Rod after quickly explaining the situation. My words were choppy, but I think he understood.

"We'd back him into his locker," Rod said, his response immediate, assertive. "One of us would stand to the right of him; one of us would stand to the left of him; and one of us would stand in front of him. We'd say, 'We're not going anywhere. We're here for you. We're not moving. You'll make it through this.'"

Those words comfort me now, as I continue to stare at the ceiling of my old bedroom. I begin to feel like that freshman in the locker room. I can actually see those players before the game, in their helmets, shoulder pads, jerseys, all standing around me. I can *feel* them around me—right here in my bedroom.

There were other times when Rod's words comforted me in the hospital. They got me to focus on the positive side of things. There were also times when Rod used a different approach to getting a message across—he pointed out the negative, sometimes in an attempt to get me past challenges I didn't even know I was facing. This was mostly back in Michigan.

⇥⇥⇤

Rod and I sat in the front seat of my Eclipse, staring at the back wall of my apartment. It was a few days before my trip to LA. As I sat, painstakingly listening to Rod rant about one of my recent stories on that chilly, early December night, I couldn't help but think of how far I'd come since graduating from Michigan. Rod knew all about my accomplishments—in education, in journalism. That's why I was baffled he was laying into me so much about a story I had written on the Michigan women's basketball team a few days earlier.

I had driven an hour to the upper edge of Ohio to watch Michigan take on the University of Toledo Lady Rockets. It was a challenge for the unproven Wolverines, going on the road to face a tough team early in the season. Toledo had recently upended powerhouse Duke on the road, which had created a lot of attention in the world of women's hoops. Yet the Wolverines destroyed the Lady Rockets, 74–46. They even opened the game with a 28–4 run, something I'd never seen them do before. In the postgame press conference, Michigan coach Sue Guevara said her players were on "business trips."

When I returned to the office, I was sure I had been inspired to write a story just as impressive and businesslike as the performance Michigan put on in Toledo. Instead, I froze. My eyes locked on the blinking cursor, and I became the proverbial deer in headlights. I was on the verge of deadline and I was stumped for a lead. Panic set in.

Just then, I recalled something Geoff Larcom, my former boss who hired me at the *News*, told me to do whenever I get into a jam like this.

"Write the first thing that comes to mind," he suggested.

So I did.

I wrote, "Wow." Actually, I wrote, "Wow. Wow! WOW!!!" as in, "*Wow*, what a show Michigan put on in Toledo!" Thankfully, the editor on the desk that night changed my lead to something a little less infantile: "If there's one word to describe Michigan's performance Thursday night against Toledo, *wow* is as close to perfect as you can get." Not an award-winner, but at least it was publishable.

"This is garbage," Rod said about the story, tossing the paper into my lap after we returned home from a friend's house.

"Garbage?" I protested.

"That's right. You could have done better than that."

"OK, it isn't Hemmingway," I thought. "But it isn't garbage, either."

"That's all you could think of?" Rod said. "'Wow'?"

"I was under deadline," I explained. "I drove from another *state*," I reminded him, thinking I should get a little leeway for those things.

"You're better than that!" Rod said, snapping those thoughts at the knees.

As we jabbed back and forth about my story, I snuck a look at the green digital numbers on the dashboard clock: 11:33. My mind wandered: More than half of *SportsCenter* down the drain! How could Rod keep going on like this? This is just one story. So I screwed it up. Big deal.

In Rod's eyes, I guess it was.

"When I played football, I had to prove myself on every play," he said. "Didn't matter what I had done the previous game, or in practice. That's how I built my reputation."

While I continued to hoist up my defenses, Rod just got louder and more aggravated, even more than I was. I tried to joust with him, but it seemed hopeless.

"Come on, man. What's the big deal?"

"It is a big deal," Rod said. He paused and looked like he was about to explode. "What's *your* story?" he asked.

Huh? What does that mean?

"What's your story?" Rod repeated in the same definite tone.

Usually Rod has some kind of closing argument. A takeaway point I call it. It's the nugget of information I'll chew over long after our conversation (or argument, in this case) has ended.

What's *my* story? My story was what we'd been talking about the previous 45 minutes.

"I'm a reporter," I told him. "I write stories every day."

"Those are other people's stories," Rod said. Suddenly he had my attention. I'd never heard my job put that way, my stories placed in that context.

"Stop watching life from the sideline," Rod said. "Get off that couch you lie on all day. Get out of the apartment and experience life. Get to know those athletes you cover."

Rod made sense, but that last part confused me: *get to know the athletes I cover?* Rod knew all about the great divide between reporters and athletes and how it's not easily, if ever, bridged. This despite the bond he and I had.

"See what makes them tick," Rod continued. "See why they do what they do. Get in their minds. Get to know them. See what it means to them, win or lose, to do what they do. You were in that locker room. What was the real story in there? If you knew, or had paid attention, you would have written more than 'wow.'"

Silence followed. I stared at the wall in front of us. Its white stucco was nearly all but gray after years of inclement weather. I felt like a child being scolded by his parent.

"Don't just watch them play then write what they do," Rod said. "Write about who they are—what their passions are, their drive, their dedication. Those things are what make the story. The score you can just plug in at the end."

Actually the score went at the top of the story or my editor would have had my hide, but I got Rod's point, only I didn't know how to apply his words, his advice. I thought I was relating to the athletes.

One reason Woodson talked to me after his drunk-driving arrest was because of how I related to him. I was dressed like a student, not the stuffy reporters on the scene that day. I think he felt he could trust me because of that and allowed himself to discuss the incident with me, which ultimately got him to open up and go on record.

I was already looking forward to the 1 a.m. *SportsCenter* when Rod and I finally got out of the car. As I walked along the dirt-and-pebble driveway, Rod followed silently behind me. It gave me a chance to think about how to use his advice.

When I got to the door, I froze just like I did when I started writing the story that caused this argument. The sight of the proverbial blank canvas of my life stopped me this time.

What's my story?
Who knows?

Rod's story, now that's easy. His story is everywhere: on the scars mapping his knees and shoulders, daily reminders of his 12 surgeries since leaving college. On his mangled fingers, all but one of the digits broken on the battlefield. And, most noticeably, on the tattoo on his left shoulder: a block *M* with a lowercase *v* and *p* underneath it.

MVP.

Most Valuable Player.

I'm reminded of the tattoo I have on my left shoulder.

A black rose.

Death.

CHAPTER NINETEEN

My New Birthday

✦

*"How you respond to the challenge in the second half
will determine what you become after the game,
whether you are a winner or a loser."*
—LOU HOLTZ

The longer City of Hope takes to find me a donor, the more my hope spirals. I think about patients remaining on donor lists for years, decades, forever. Luckily, I don't need a heart or a liver, just a Good Samaritan, like Rod. I need another angel to swoop down and help me, even though he or she doesn't even know me.

While I'm still sidelined from the game of life, I'm able to take some comfort in my daily conversations with Rod. With nothing new to deal with regarding my illness, Rod and I start talking about his situation, his problems. More times than not, the conversations give me a purpose because they become less and less about me.

As long as I've known Rod, he's been a "Super Bowl champion." He's been riding the wave of the greatest victory known to man, the highest-rated TV program of the year. And what does Rod have to show for his ultimate victory, other than a humongous ring he wears everywhere? I've never asked him, but the somberness in his voice explains a lot.

"Not much," Rod tells me when I ask him what's been happening back home.

"What do you mean not much?"

"Not much, bro. Just hanging out."

"Where?"

"Frazier's, the Building, out with friends." Frazier's, I recall, is an out-of-the-way sports bar Rod once took me to, where, like Norm from *Cheers*, everybody knows his name.

It's the same story at the Building, where Rod is (and always will be, I presume) a hero. A lot of the young players there—and Rod has told me this on more than one occasion—believe capturing the ring (i.e., the glory, the fame) is the ultimate goal. It no longer represents the validation of a mission based on teamwork, like it's always been for Rod. Their idol is the jewelry, not the game, not the mission.

"That's the problem with the players these days," Rod says. "It's not about the tradition anymore, or the team. Everybody's out there running around, doing their own thing."

I remember a story Rod told me about a freshman running back doing just that. "This guy just scored a touchdown; I think it was his first. We ran up to him in the end zone, just like we do for everybody who scores, and he ran away from us! He took his helmet off and started running around the field like a fool, yelling to the fans. Man, when he came back to the bench, we all got in his face. We said, 'Listen! We're a *team*. When you score, you wait until we all come over and congratulate you. Next time we see you running around like that again, you won't ever get another play called for you at Michigan. You got that?"

"What was the player's reaction?" I asked Rod.

"He was like, 'I didn't know, I'm sorry. I won't do it again.' He was sniffling, almost in tears."

Nowadays, Rod doesn't have that kind of influence over the younger players. He can tell them what to do, how to act, but it doesn't sink in like it used to. I know this gets to him. Combine that with the itch Rod still has to be on the field and things have to be overwhelming for him.

— ·— ≡✦≡ —· —

With nothing new to capitalize on following his retirement, it seems like Rod really is back in college, not just hanging out in his old college town. It's like he's just starting out. What's worse, he's doing it without all of his old teammates or his new one, me.

Even during this time of transition—the first real unknown of his life—Rod makes it a point to keep everyone back home abreast of my progress.

Head coach Lloyd Carr, in fact, sent me a get-well card after hearing the news. The return address simply read, "Schembechler Hall—A-Squared, Michigan." It reminded me of when someone addresses a letter to the president to "White House, Washington, D.C.," or when a child sends a note to Santa Claus at the "North Pole."

Although Rod is still helping me during my plight by spreading word of my illness, I know he wants to do more. The wife of Louis XIV, Madame De Maintenon, wrote, "The true way to soften one's troubles is to solace those of others." Rod must have been doing just that for me during the six months before I got sick. Maybe he had his own troubles then and alleviated them by helping me with mine.

The biggest problem Rod had? Since early in our friendship, it was obvious Rod was disappointed about not being able to play football anymore.

One day in my apartment, just before the start of the last NFL season, Rod and I were working on a story, some ideas for our children's book—*The Adventures of Tyrone Butterfield*, we're calling it—when Rod's cell phone rang. It was some of his former Ravens teammates. They were driving from Baltimore to New York for a preseason game against the Giants. Whatever they were telling Rod made him laugh like he had never heard anything as funny.

When Rod hung up, he was still smiling, still laughing. But I could tell a wave of regret had just washed over him. Clearly, Rod wanted to be in that car with his teammates, not with me in my apartment.

All this time later, I try to help my troubles by helping Rod with his. Any problems I have throwing out the trash, cleaning up the apartment, or waiting anxiously for a donor, I stop complaining about. (I'll save that for Mom.)

Rod's latest problem involves his living arrangement. He's moved out of the one place of stability he's been in since he retired: the Ecklers' house in Chelsea. It's too far from his car-customizing company, too far in general from Ann Arbor, where everything is happening. So he found a house near campus to rent. It's a less-than-spacious downtown abode he shares with a friend.

I ask Rod about his friend.

"You've never met the guy," he tells me and offers little else about him. I don't press the issue. Instead, Rod shares how uncomfortable he's been in the house. He laments there are no screens in the windows in his bedroom and that mosquitoes are coming in at night.

"Just get some new screens," I tell him.

"It's not just that, bro. It's not a real home. I need to be able to come home at night and chill out, not worry about anything—a place that's mine. I haven't felt that way since I left for college. That's almost 10 years."

As I look around my mom's apartment, it's clear I'm not where I want to be either. I guess Rod and I are both in need of solacing.

I try to change the subject.

"Why don't you go back on the radio?" I ask. Rod had recently left the station, for reasons I never really understood. I remember him telling me he asked the producers for more money and they declined. Then there was that lack of communication that kept him off the game day–morning telecasts. It seemed that no one at the station was ever on the same page with Rod, which I'm sure aggravated him to no end.

From Rod's groan, it appears returning to the radio is not such a good idea.

Inevitably, our talks end the same.

"When are you coming home?" he'll ask.

"I don't know. It's too hard to tell," I say.

Still Rod persists. He explains the benefits of returning to Michigan, of being together again, of regaining the momentum we had before I got sick. Rod reminds me of our many projects, including a magazine we want to start up. It will feature hard-hitting viewpoints from professional athletes on the latest sports topics—not the cookie-cutter stuff they usually feed mainstream media. We also have plans to write a book of short stories, and that children's book.

"You said Nana always wanted you to write a children's book," Rod says. "You gonna let her down?"

Sometimes it seems Rod has forgotten I'm actually waiting for a bone marrow transplant. This isn't some injury that will heal in time. I don't know when my problem will go away, when my donor will be found. Despite how much I want to do everything Rod and I had planned, I don't know when I'll get back to where I was—physically, mentally, or emotionally.

There's another reason I can't tell Rod when I'm coming home. It's because I don't know if I even want to. This is whether I find a donor or not.

How can I?

I can barely walk down the block: it's like running a marathon for me. I still carry around a dribble glass, although I don't need it as much anymore. I still have trouble eating, so I haven't gained back much weight. And on top of everything else, now I have problems going to the bathroom. Without getting into details, either it doesn't come out—or it *really* comes out.

What I find most shocking is that Mom is taking care of me these days like I'm a baby. She does physical therapy with me—range-of-motion exercises—to strengthen my legs. While I lie in bed, she pushes my knees up to my chest, then down again, over and over, so my legs don't atrophy.

These are all matters I have to think about. Thus, while I try to lift Rod up by giving him hope that we will continue with all of our plans,

I still wonder: will I ever get back to where I was physically? Can I do without the constant care of my mom and nearby doctor? Dr. Snyder, in fact, said he likes his patients to live close to the hospital for the first year after the transplant. A full year!

My concern about the future wears on me, day after day, until Dr. Snyder walks into the examining room during one of my outpatient visits and tells Mom and I that we have good news. After three months of searching, we've found a donor.

Three, actually.

⋯ ✠ ⋯

It's May 4, 2002, a little after 3 a.m, and I'm in the bone marrow unit at City of Hope, receiving a bag of blood, my donor's blood, and I'm not throwing a temper tantrum. Dr. Snyder says my Good Samaritan is a 34-year-old woman from Dottinger, Germany. Annette Lechler is her name. She's a mother of two and around my age, which makes her a better fit than the other two donors. Also, Annette is a six-of-six preliminary match—compatible at every molecular level. (Two additional blood tests show her to be a 24-of-24 match.) It really is a miracle, Dr. Snyder says. Because I have no siblings, there was a fear I'd never find a perfect match.

During the transfusion, Mom takes pictures as I flash a smile as big as I've ever had. She and Nana have their own smiles as I hold up the jumbo 3 from the tear-off calendar on the wall. The transplant was scheduled for the 3rd, but the woman City of Hope sent to Germany to pick up my blood didn't land at LAX until well after midnight. At any rate, I've been ripping sheets off this calendar each morning in anticipation of this day.

We got here a few days ago, when I started preparing for the transplant. That meant getting my immune system to where it needs to be: gone.

I'm still not at the toughest part of the transplant. That'll be during the isolation stage, when people will have to dress like Gene Wilder in *Young Frankenstein* before entering the room. But I am confident in my chances. It's because I know I'm on the final leg of my marathon ride back to health. I can see the finish line now, even though a nurse who prepped me for the transplant said this is going to be the hardest thing I'll ever have to go through. Even with that prediction, I manage to sport a Cheshire grin as Mom snaps away on the camera.

Thomas Paine wrote, "I love the man that can smile in trouble, that can gather strength from distress and grow brave by reflection." Why not smile?

Everybody who has helped me during this trying experience is here with me, if only in spirit. They include my family members who sent me get-well cards and phoned me in the other hospital; people at City of Hope who have supported me (especially the woman who flew all the way to Germany just to pick up my blood); and all those in Michigan: friends, coworkers, strangers—they're all here with me. So is Rod—we talked earlier—as well as that angel 6,500 miles away who sat for hours donating her blood for me. I feel her in the room the most.

"My *donor*," I say as I watch her blood go from the bag into my chest, where my catheter port is now. "I have a *donor*."

Something else makes me smile on this special day—my new birthday, nurses tell me. I'm officially on the clock. If all goes well during the transplant, which takes four to five weeks on average, Dr. Snyder says, I'll begin a 100-day, at-home recovery phase that will include three or four outpatient visits a week. If tests look good then— another bone marrow biopsy will be needed, which I'm not looking forward to—I can pack my bags and go home.

Could that mean home to Michigan, where I once ventured in the fall of 1998 in anticipation of all the good that lay ahead, even though I had never stepped foot in the state before? I still don't know. I have only done the math in my head to figure out the time frame for when I can return to my old life. I don't know if anything else will come up that will require me to stay near the hospital when the transplant's over.

Dr. Snyder says complications are possible, but he doesn't seem overly concerned about it. One of Dr. Snyder's other patients, however, feels I shouldn't get too excited.

"Don't be surprised if you have to go back to the hospital after the transplant," says the patient, now a volunteer at City of Hope. "I went back 16 times after my transplant, for fevers and bad rashes and—" I shut him out. I have chosen not to focus on the problems that may arise. I shall keep my eye on the prize, as I once heard Johnny Cochran say. Or, in the words of Henry Ford, I will trust that "obstacles are those frightful things you see when you take your eyes off your goal."

My goal is to regain that momentum I had in life, whether it brings me back to Michigan, to my career and friendship with Rod, or to a new life back here, in LA. Whatever happens, I want to find the answer to Rod's question, the one he asked me so explosively that chilly December night behind my apartment, it was as if life itself hung in the balance.

"What's *your* story?"

I'm starting to think it's being written right now—in my donor's blood.

CHAPTER TWENTY

Test Flight Home

⊶ ⊯◈⊨ ⊷

"The rewards for those who persevere far exceed
the pain that must precede the victory."
—TED W. ENGSTROM

With my donor's blood circulating through my body, I can at least give Rod an idea of when I can come home. Next time I see Dr. Snyder, I'll press him for a potential return date.

"Well, there are a lot of factors," Dr. Snyder says, when he checks in on me before going home for the night.

"Ballpark," I tell him.

"I would say . . . late summer. You can probably go back then."

"Late summer it is," I say, closing the deal. That night, I call Rod to give him the news.

"Cool," he says, then tells me he'll start looking for a place for us to stay. Rod seems so excited about my returning home, I don't tell him I haven't yet made the decision.

I hope that's the right move.

It's early September 2002. Mom drives me to LAX, where I will board a flight for the life cancer tried to take away from me. Five hours later, I touch down at Detroit Metro Airport. Dusk has fallen. As the plane taxis toward to the terminal, the runway lights flicker on.

After all I've been through the last nine months, I can't help but think the lights are spelling out a message to me: WELCOME HOME, STEVE. I smile at the thought. It makes me think I've made the right decision to leave Los Angeles. My smile dims quickly when I realize I haven't actually made that decision yet.

This trip is just a trial run, approved by Dr. Snyder to see if I can handle being away from the safety net of my mom's apartment and nearby doctor. This will be my first real physical excursion since I was diagnosed, and it's already challenging—physically and emotionally. Luckily, this is nothing new to me: I remember how difficult it was just rejoining society for the first time when I finally got the OK to leave the house.

I went on my first excursion near the end of the 100-day recovery phase. Mom and I drove up the street to the corner grocery store I worked at in high school. Dr. Snyder had told me I could be around people as long as I wore a mask and stayed away from crowds. Everything was going well until a guy pushed his cart down the same aisle we were in. I became nervous at the sight of him steering that wobbly cart, which to me looked like a Mack truck. I took a step back, then another, until my shoulder blades were flush with the canned goods. I held my breath until the driver of the truck passed.

I feel a little of that same terror now as the plane rolls into the gate. People look at me as they deboard. They see my mask—I still have to wear it in certain situations, like this one because of all the bacteria-filled air circulating in the cabin.

After I exit the plane—I'm the last one to leave, not waiting to get caught up in the stampede of passengers—I begin the long journey to baggage claim. I stop and sit down along the way to catch my breath.

People are still looking at me; I forgot to take off my mask. I snatch it off my face and jam it into my backpack.

Stepping off an escalator at the end of the new terminal at Detroit Metro—it features a tunnel with animated neon lights that change color as you walk through it (from blue to red to green)—I spot Rod. He's at the other end of the baggage claim, about three carousels away, but he's never looked bigger. Or more impressive.

Rod's dressed in loose-fitting jeans, white tennis shoes, and a blue-and-white-striped dress shirt. Hanging from his neck is a picture ID tag from the Ann Arbor–area high school he now teaches at. He's a special education teacher—Mr. Payne, the kids call him. Rod also told me he has plans to coach the football team someday. The principal there, a former Michigan football player, is probably going to be making a change at the helm, as the team hasn't been very good lately. At least that's how I recall the story. Rod still is not a fan of offering details.

When we meet, Rod and I hug like we did in the hospital when he first came to visit. This time it feels like we're soldiers returning home from war. Victorious.

"It's good to see you, bro."

"You too," I say.

After fetching my bag, we step into Rod's high-riding truck. It's parked outside at the curb—MVP parking. In moments, we set off on the satisfying, oh-so-familiar drive to Ann Arbor. It's a beautiful day in Detroit, the smell of summer still in the air. I can feel the sun on my skin, a breeze on my face. It feels like I'm a prisoner seeing the light of day for the first time in years.

While I'm grateful to have made it back here, I know I'm still not home yet. Not until it *feels* like I'm home, like it's my purpose to be here. That's how I felt when I first traveled this road via taxi, when I was checking out colleges in the summer of 1998.

I flew straight from the University of North Carolina in Chapel Hill, having already toured the University of Southern California's campus. SC never had a chance: too close to home. And once I saw Michigan's campus, UNC didn't have a chance either.

"You all right?" Rod asks as we coast along I-94 once again.

"Great," I say, deciding to keep my indecision secret. "How can I not be?"

⊶ ⋈⊹≣ ⊷

Despite the progress I've made since that first trip to the grocery store, I am still weary throughout this visit. Consequently, even though each day provides clues about why I should return to Michigan—such as the standing ovation I get from my coworkers during my first appearance in the newsroom—I am still reluctant to make that leap of faith. That's exactly what it is: a leap—clear across the country—at a time when I can't even cross the room without getting winded.

I wonder if I can return to the newspaper business, the constant pressure of the job. Will it be like it was before, consuming every minute of my day? How can I commit to this move when I can't even walk up a flight of stairs without a struggle? And from what Rod tells me, the place he found for us to rent has an outside stairwell longer and steeper than mine in LA. We'll be renting the top floor of an early-twentieth-century house, Rod says.

"You'll get used to them," he tells me when I share my concern about the stairs.

At Jessica's apartment later, Rod starts describing the amenities of the house, like he's a real estate agent. I'm staying with Jessica, who's been patiently awaiting my return, and her roommate, Shannon, during the weeklong visit. When I arrived, they had a "WELCOME HOME, STEVE" sign on the wall—a real one, not like the one I imagined on the runway.

"There's a giant outdoor deck. We can barbecue there," Rod says as he skewers some top sirloin and potatoes he's about to toss onto Jessica's grill. "It's got three rooms, and it's in a good location—close to all the action, but not too close. We'll go by there tomorrow so you can see it."

"I don't know," I say, starting to feel a little trapped. "It's kind of hard for me to get around."

"You just got on a plane and flew all the way here," Rod reminds me as he positions the kabobs on the grill.

Rod has a point but not enough to make me do cartwheels while thinking about the move.

"It's like I told you before the transplant," Rod says. "That same faith that got you where you are now will carry you the rest of the way."

"What if something goes wrong?" I ask him. "Faith is one thing, bro. Cancer is another. What about all these medications I'm taking? How will I get those? My mom's been giving them to me each day. I don't even know what they are." For this trip, in fact, Mom packed my pills in plastic lunch bags—one bag for each day.

This decision I need to make consumes my thoughts. I even think about it while I cover a Michigan football game—the season opener. The University of Washington is in town, and I'm freelancing for the *Seattle P-I*. At halftime, I joke with a fellow reporter that I find this day so amazing: Despite my illness, and all the uncertainty of it, I manage not to miss even one Michigan football game. "Couldn't have worked out better if I'd planned it," I say to the guy as we help ourselves to the tasty Michigan Stadium dogs with kraut and relish in the press box.

Even with the return of my appetite, I am still unsure about the move. Maybe I can just stay home, keep doing those stories for the *LA Times*. Maybe even get a job there. That's how I was hired at the *Ann Arbor News*: freelancing stories for them while I was still in college.

"I'm glad you've found a place for us to live," I tell Rod when we meet up after the game. (Michigan beat Washington on a last-second field goal in front of 111,491 fans, most of which seemed to flood into downtown afterward.) Then I confess, "And I know you thought I was going to come back here ever since we found the donor. But I'm not sure now. It just feels weird not being near the hospital and my doctor."

"Then find a hospital near here," Rod says. "Meet the doctors there."

I follow Rod's advice Monday morning. Jessica takes a few hours off from work, and we drive to a local hospital, another university research facility. It doesn't take long before I discover it's no City of Hope.

The doctor we meet, the head of oncology there, starts arguing with me when I tell him I can't recite the dozen post-transplant medications I'm taking.

"How can you not know?" he asks.

"My mom takes care of all that for me."

"You *have* to know the meds you're taking." The doctor becomes frantic. He's searching through the paperwork I just filled out in the waiting room. To try to calm him, so we can finally start talking about my situation, my potential move here, I start to rattle off some of my medications.

"I take Prednisone, the steroids—um, Diflucan—"

"I need to know all of the medications and the dosages you take," the doctor says, not letting me continue the list. (Good thing, 'cause that's all I know.)

"Look, they're all in my file," I say. "I'll get you that. I just wanted to come down here and meet you so I know who I can see for my checkups if I move here." By the time we leave, Jessica is in tears. Later, I make sure to tell Rod all about my trip to the local hospital.

"Why would I leave everything I have at my disposal in LA for that?"

"Look, man, I told you: you have to have faith. Find another doctor."

"That was the head of oncology!"

Eventually, having heard enough of my indecision, Rod sets aside his nurturing tone. At a bar and grill with friends one night, Rod pulls me aside. We walk to the tables near the back bar, by the dartboards and pool tables. The place reeks of beer. It makes me want to throw up.

"We need to talk, bro," Rod says, taking a seat at a table. "We need to get some things straight. Team meeting." I cringe. I've never done well in team meetings with Rod. Probably because they're held when I've done something wrong. My defenses immediately go up.

"You were in Michigan before you got sick," Rod begins. "You belong in Michigan after too. Don't let what happened to you dictate your life." Rod then reminds me of his many surgeries, how his first inclination at the time was to turn around and go home—home to

Mom, to the comfort of his own bed, friends, and extended family members.

"And how would I have turned out had I done that?" Rod says, his eyes drilling into mine. "You think I would have accomplished any of those things I did?" He unlocks his eyes from me and shoots a look at his ring, as if to say, "See—my point exactly."

I know Rod means business because he's just pulled out the Super Bowl–ring card. Usually Rod downplays the jewelry, to the extent that when people ask him about it, he sometimes tells them he got it out of a Cracker Jack box.

"Plus," Rod says. "You've been so focused on your own issues, you've forgotten about the team."

"What do you mean?" I snap back. "I'm here, aren't I?"

"Yeah, you're here. But suiting up for the game and playing are two different things." This starts to feels like the conversation we had behind my apartment, when I had no idea why he was badgering me so much about my women's basketball story.

"I didn't move into another place because you told me you were coming back," Rod says, leaning over the table so he doesn't have to get loud. "I was waiting for you, so we could get a place together and continue all the things we were doing before you got sick. And now you tell me you want to stay back there?"

I'm starting to get it. He's right: I never thought about that.

"It's time for you to help keep this momentum we have—*you* have—going," Rod says. "Look, I love you like a brother, and I'll always do anything for you. But there's also a side of me that feels I've done everything I can for you. If you stay in LA, you'll lose everything you've been working for since you left that apartment you lived in all those years—your whole life! There was a reason you left LA in the first place. You're the one who told me that. Remember?"

When we rejoin our group—it's so large, we had to push tables together—I suddenly have a lot on my mind. For the rest of the evening, I sit silently. I just want to go home and be alone. I'm hardly in the mood for a party.

Following my trip to Michigan, I really do feel alone back at Mom's apartment. The solitude helps me realize how much I reconnected with Ann Arbor. I start to believe that my fears of returning to my old job—and to Rod's scrutiny—are far less daunting than knowing I never had what it took to try. I realize I have no choice—I *have* to go back. If it doesn't work out, I can always come home. I just know I can't be a cancer patient forever.

Later that day, I call Rod. "Sign the lease," I tell him.

"Let's ride," he says, hardly sounding surprised at my decision.

Something tells me Rod knew I'd make the right move all along.

⋅—⋅ ≼◆≽ ⋅—⋅

Two weeks later, on a brilliantly sunny day in Los Angeles, I board a plane headed for the life that cancer tried to take away from me. Again.

Rod picks me up from the airport, and we make the familiar drive along I-94 to Ann Arbor. This time we stop just short of town, in Ypsilanti, Ann Arbor's sister city. This is where Rod found the house for us to rent, right across the street from Eastern Michigan University.

With the bustle of Detroit long behind us, it feels like the last nine months didn't happen. I see the green landscape ahead and all those evergreen trees dotting the highway. They're what first convinced me this is where I wanted to go to college.

As I expected, things are difficult at first. I have nightmares every night due to all the medications I'm on, the steroids and immunosuppressant drugs. The steroids, coupled with all the morphine I took in the hospital, used to give me bad hallucinations— from numbers dancing on the clock to visions of mercenaries coming into my room at night to kill me. I will take upward of 25 pills a day for the next five years—or more—to help regulate my blood counts until my body can do it on its own.

The nightmares wake me at all hours, leaving me breathless and in a cold sweat. This happened a lot during the transplant and in the three months of recovery that followed. Despite all the soggy T-shirts I whip into the hamper each morning—I sometimes go through two or three a night—I still feel like a new man: reborn, recharged, invigorated.

Yet, I also resort to my old habits much of the time. When Rod arrives home from work, he sees a familiar sight: me prone on the couch, wearing the same clothes I slept in.

"What's going on?" Rod asks. "Did you stay there all day?" At least I have a doctor's blessing to do it now. During my last visit to City of Hope, Dr. Snyder instructed me to "listen to my body."

"He said some days I'll be fine," I tell Rod. "And other days I'll feel extremely fatigued—for three or four days straight. There's nothing I can do about it." (I still have to fly back to LA every three months for checkups to regulate this very thing.)

"Whatever, man," Rod says, scooting me over on the couch. I stretch out like a cat waking up from a long nap.

"When are you going back to work?" he asks.

I don't answer.

"What a day," Rod groans, stretching out like I did and taking up about three quarters of the couch in the process. "What are you watching?"

"I don't know—I mean about going back to work. This is the History Channel, underwater shipwrecks. I'm switching between CNN and ESPN, but they're both on commercial."

Rod asks again when I plan to go back to work.

"I'm still getting used to this new area. I'd rather wait until I'm ready before I start driving around, covering sporting events."

Even driving a car is still a challenge to me. My Eclipse, which has been in storage since I called Rod and told him I wasn't coming home, really does feel like a spaceship now. I feel uncomfortable around the controls, like I'm careering through space, not driving along Washtenaw Avenue, the street we now live on.

While I enjoy this well-deserved R&R, I know my first order of business should be to reconnect with work. I should at least give my bosses an update of my progress. They have always said they'd have my job waiting for me when I come back.

One day, when Rod gets home from work, he finds me on the couch and asks me if I want to go with him to my storage unit. He's been using it to stash some of his things since I've been gone.

"And we have to get your stuff," Rod says. "You ready to go?"

A short time later, Rod and I gather up my boxes and toss them into his truck. I notice they're heavier than I expected. I guess Rod didn't throw out everything during the packing party he had at my apartment after he learned I was sick. I remember the occasion well: I coordinated it from my hospital room. Jessica was there, along with Shannon, and my new roommate, Kevin, a former Pi Kappa Phi fraternity brother who moved in after Arun started living with his girlfriend in his senior year.

"Jessica said you dipped into my change jar when you packed up my stuff," I tell Rod on the way home. "What's up with that?"

"Shoot, I never did that," Rod says, trying to mask his grin.

"So she just made it up? I don't think so."

"Here," Rod says, scooping some change from his ashtray. "Take this."

"Oh, 37 cents. Thanks."

"I needed some quarters for the parking meters," Rod says. "I just took a couple bucks."

"Parking meters? What happened to MVP parking?"

When we get back to the house, I load the boxes into my tiny corner bedroom with the vaulted ceiling. (Rod has the big bedroom near the kitchen.) The boxes are filled with clothes I don't remember owning. Most of the garments are folded nicely (probably Jessica's handiwork), and others simply tossed rag-tag into the box (Rod, maybe Kevin—no, definitely Rod). But they're all here: every garment I thought I had lost along with the rest of my life back here. It's like Christmas morning, much better than how I spent the one previous.

I start to arrange the clothes neatly across my bed, like I did all of the toys and sports memorabilia Dad bought me during our shopping sprees in Minnesota each summer. I stand proudly over my new wardrobe, even though none of the clothes fit me anymore. I immediately get choked up; it reminds me of when I put on my leather jacket when I checked out of the hospital. These emotional swings continue for the next few days, until I eventually fall back into the schedule I had before I got sick.

One overcast morning I leap off the couch and decide I'm strong enough to reconnect with work. I have to—I can't sit here forever.

"Are you ready to meet with me?" I ask my boss after scanning the top of the sports section for his phone number. I can't believe I forgot it.

I show up at the office at 9:30 the following morning, half expecting another standing ovation from my coworkers. When I don't get it—just one ovation per disease, I guess—I feel relieved: this is just like before, when I came to work and nobody gave a hoot. Intriguing phenomenon: until you go back to work, back to what you did prior to getting sick—driving, doing laundry, grocery shopping, even playing tennis like I did a few times—then you're not really cured. It takes more than a doctor's OK to get you back to the game of life.

After a quick greeting with my boss and a few questions from him about my health, we get down to business. This is the *Ann Arbor News'* third sports editor since I was hired in October 1999. He tells me that my old job—the weekly College Notes section, along with the teams I covered as part of the job (women's basketball, softball, gymnastics, field hockey), is not available. The reporter placed in charge of it after my vacation became indefinite is too settled into the position to be displaced.

"Steve, we have something special for you," my boss says, giving me no time to think about how I've just been bumped.

Special? That actually sounds nice.

"We're creating new weekly editions of the paper, and we want you to head up the sports section in the inaugural one. It's called the *Ypsilanti Community News.*"

It's my "news sense," my new boss says, and that I'm a "self-starter" that led him and his bosses to pick me for the job.

"You'll have to be on top of things a lot more in this position," he tells me. "You'll be at a new office, over in Ypsi, and you'll have to make a lot of your own decisions."

This is just what I've always wanted: responsibility, freedom to do things the way I feel comfortable doing them. And best of all, no more calls from the assistant sports editor asking where my stories are. Plus, I'm told this will be a one-person sports staff. I'll wear the hat of editor, writer, columnist, copy editor, and ombudsman—the person who deals with grievances of readers. Hopefully I won't have to wear that hat too often.

"This will be your baby," my boss says. "Raise it well."

"Will do," I say. "You can count on me."

My first week on the job is tiresome. I arrive at work early and hit the phones all day, trying to create a database of sources and contacts. This is just in preparation for the paper's kickoff, slated for a few weeks from now, in early November. At that time, I'll have to write four stories for each edition, including a column and a calendar of upcoming events.

Despite my enthusiasm for my new job, I'm so exhausted when I get home from work I immediately collapse on the couch. After a while, to my surprise, I find Rod sitting next to me, dog-tired after his day. He seems more emotionally tired, though.

"I can't take all this bull at school," he says. The strain in his voice is unbecoming of him.

"It's not like a football team, where everyone has the same goal," he adds. "Learning institutions are different. The bickering between teachers about teaching tactics and who's getting what classes in the fall—they're a constant thorn."

There's something else, I notice, that's bringing Rod down. It's that he's required to do things at work I'm sure were never explained in his contract. Not even in small print.

Before going to work recently, I visited Rod. As I approached his classroom, I heard some commotion coming from down the hall. I turned around and saw a security guard chasing a student. They were dodging the students who had just gotten out of class. Seeing the boy running toward me, I backed up. Rod, unaware of what was happening, walked out of his class to greet me. As the kid ran by us, Rod scooped him into the air, intercepting him like a giant football.

"All in a day's work?" I asked Rod as the kid kicked and screamed from atop his shoulders.

"Pretty much," Rod said, handing him back to the security guard.

—+ ≡✦≡ +—

Despite the annoyances of our jobs, Rod and I are happy to be together again, back to the way things were. Yet we still need more time to get used to these major changes in our lives.

Rod and I deal with our frazzled emotions in different ways. I tend to keep them inside, whereas Rod lets them out. While we know we always have each other's backs, very soon, like real brothers, we start to get on each other's nerves. It makes for a combustible chemistry in the house.

"You gonna knock those dishes out today," Rod asks just about every time he heads out the door in the morning.

"Isn't it your turn?" I say, getting in some couch time before I go to work.

"I'm tellin' you—it's your turn!"

"Forget the dishes," I tell Rod. "We need money for rent."

"I'm waiting on a check."

"You're always waiting on a check. What's the deal over there?"

"Man, I'm on top of it. I'll have the cash for you by the time you knock those dishes out."

"I told you it's your turn!" I say.

Rod slams the door and stomps down the stairs.

The tension between us builds in proportion to the dishes, until everything comes crashing down one night. Rod and I are having a shouting match in our narrow, gingerbread house–sized kitchen. It begins with the dishes and escalates to include a medley of different grievances. We're face-to-face, or jaw-to-forehead more like it, when I take a plate of food I'm about to eat and throw it on the floor by Rod's feet. Then I storm out of the house, crossing the street into EMU's parking lot. After pacing in the parking lot for 20 minutes, I return home to find the mess I made in the kitchen is still there.

"You cooled down now?" Rod asks, walking out of his bedroom.

"Yeah," I say, then get down on the floor to start cleaning up.

Without being asked, Rod pitches in to help.

"Now what am I going to eat?" I wonder aloud, feeling much better that we've resolved our issues. "I'm thinking about getting some White Castles." I loved going to White Castle in Minnesota with Dad; I practically grew up on them. I always hated that there weren't any in LA. "You want me to pick you up any?" I ask Rod.

"No way, bro. I'm training."

"Not me," I say, hustling out the door, hoping they're open.

CHAPTER TWENTY-ONE

Are You Guys Rappers?

"It's what you choose to learn after
you know it all that really matters."
—UNKNOWN

od and I soon focus our pent-up energy on our creative discussions. Our goal is to get serious about them again, get back to the days when I'd rush to my laptop as soon as Rod brought up an interesting topic to talk about. We're serious enough to decide to purchase a desk for the third room of our house, which will be our office. There will be no distractions there. No TV, no friends dropping by, and no couch to chill out on.

Late one afternoon, Rod and I drive across town to Art Van, a popular furniture store in Ann Arbor. There, in addition to meeting a salesman named Art—Art from Art Van, we get a kick out of that—we find a gem: an L-shaped desk with a drawer for the keyboard and a shelf on one side.

While waiting in line to pay for the desk, I notice a few customers in line start to recognize Rod. One of them, an elderly gentleman, asks Rod what he's been up to since college, and what he thinks of the current Michigan football team. The scene is familiar; I saw this a lot before I got sick.

"I was in the league, but I'm retired now," Rod says.

"That's right," the gray-haired gentleman responds. "You played for the Ravens, right?"

Maybe he read that in the story I wrote about Rod after we met.

"I first played for Cincinnati, then the Ravens," Rod says, towering over the man and his silver-haired wife standing proudly beside him.

"I remember that game when you broke your hand," the man says, pointing up at Rod. "That was the most amazing thing I'd ever seen!" The old man is referring to the Northwestern game Rod's junior year. He broke his right wrist in the first half, got it taped up at halftime, and snapped the ball the rest of the game (and season) with his left hand.

As the admirers grow, so does their appreciation for Rod's accomplishments. One fellow, a young man, maybe in his mid-30s, places his newborn baby in Rod's arms. I think, "What, is Rod a politician now?" What shocks me even more, the father then grabs his cell phone and enthusiastically tells the person on the other end—his wife I'm guessing—who's holding the little tyke. It seems he couldn't be more excited about Rod coochie-cooing his future Michigan football player.

As the admirers continue to grow, Rod answers each of their questions dutifully and cheerfully. There's the elderly couple, the father, a pair of teenage girls, some nondescript furniture shoppers, an employee of the store, and more. When I approach the counter, I notice even the young blonde girl at the cash register is paying close attention to the scene behind me. She can barely focus on what she's doing.

"Are you guys rappers?" she asks me as I take out my wallet.

Is she joking? I study her face. Her perplexed look tells me she isn't. While searching for my credit card, I try to come up with something witty to say in response to her question.

"No," I tell her, handing her my credit card. "I'm the rapper. *He's* my bodyguard." As Rod and I leave the store—the desk to be delivered later—I notice Rod is staring at the pavement as he walks slowly across the parking lot. He appears to be in deep thought.

I have to know what caused that scene. While it's hardly unusual for folks to recognize Rod, it's never been like this.

Rappers? Are you kidding?

"What was that all about?" I ask.

Rod doesn't respond. I'm about to ask again when he suddenly speaks up.

"Whenever I stepped on that field, bro," Rod says, staring at the pavement and perhaps into his past, "I played to inspire."

The second I hear those words, a chill shoots down my spine. The sound of the rush-hour traffic disappears.

I suddenly realize that Rod didn't do all those unselfish things for me over the past year because I'm such a great guy. He does them for everybody. I just happened to be the one who needed them the most.

The months go by quickly after our trip to Art Van. Meanwhile, my job continues to consume me, though not like before. I'm working smarter now, not harder. And since I'm the point man for the new community sports section, I'm connecting with people more than I ever have.

I wrote a story on the local VFW, and now I know World War II and Vietnam veterans. I did a story on a popular after-school sports program at a local high school, and now I know teachers, motivators, coaches. Not the Lloyd Carr and Brian Billick kind of coaches, but those at the grassroots level—the kind you can go out and have a beer with, get to know.

The only price I pay for this success at work is that Rod and I don't get to renew our creative discussions as much as we'd like to. We do, however, get along just as well as we ever have. It feels like Rod and I are becoming less like friends and more like real brothers. And since you don't hang out with your brother every day, I started spending more time with Jessica.

I'd put our relationship on hold for so long it was time to reconnect. We had fun together, got to know each other more. I love her family, most of whom live in Mount Pleasant, where Jessica graduated from Central Michigan University. But we soon realized we weren't made for each other, like we had hoped.

"Don't worry, bro," Rod says, when I share the news about Jessica. "When it all comes crashing down, you know who to turn to."

"Very funny," I tell him, but it's a relief to know our status either way. For a while, when I was in LA, it was up in the air, like everything else in my life.

Maybe a year after Rod and I move into our early-twentieth-century house, Rod comes home from work one day and drops a bomb on me.

"Bro, I'm joining the Marines."

"Bad day at the office?" I ask. With what goes on at that school, it's almost as if Rod is already in the Marines.

"No joke, bro. I'm meeting with a placement officer this weekend."

"What about all your injuries?"

"I've been training, and they feel pretty good. I'm getting ready for their physical. That's why I've been on the liquid diet lately. If I pass that, I'll be in."

"Aren't you too old?"

"Nope."

I've known Rod has always been an enthusiast of guns and knives and battle. I also know that a lot of the men in the Payne family, including Rod's father, a Vietnam veteran, served in some branch of the U.S. military. Still, I'm surprised it's come to this.

"Is it because of school?" I ask Rod, alluding to the daily shenanigans with unruly students and the childlike jealousy from teachers. From what little Rod has told me about the situation, some of them think he shouldn't have a direct line to the soon-to-be-vacant head football coaching position.

"Nah, I'm not worried about that," Rod says.

"Then what?"

"You know me. I miss the hierarchy. I miss getting up each day and having that mission." That explains it all. Only I can't see him getting past the pain in his knees.

Before I got sick, I remember Rod and I were preparing to watch a movie one night at my apartment when he knelt down to retrieve a video off a bottom-level shelf and froze. He had to put one arm on the shelf for balance and slowly lower himself to the carpet.

"Bro, there was a time in the league when I couldn't even do this," he said, resting on a knee as he gazed in my direction. "If I had played another year, I don't think I could ever have done this again."

"I know you're stronger now," I tell Rod, still trying to get my head around him becoming one of the few, the proud. "But can your knees really handle the stress?"

"We'll see."

While Rod trains every day after work, including running like a cross-country athlete on the weekends, I start searching for a new job. I first thought I'd stay in Ypsilanti, find another roommate. But then I figured maybe Rod's move is a sign for me to move on too.

I scour the journalism Web sites and find a posting for a full-time sports reporter at the *Arizona Daily Sun*, a Pulitzer-owned newspaper in Flagstaff, right off historic Route 66. The job description says I'll have a chance to cover all of the professional sports teams in Arizona: the Suns, Diamondbacks, Cardinals, Coyotes—even the Mercury, the WNBA team. Pro sports—just what I've always wanted to do, and what I *need* to do if I want to advance in this profession. That's what the employment recruiter at the *LA Times* told me before saying I should call back in five years if I want to work there. So I send off a cover letter and portfolio immediately.

A week and a half later, on a trip to LA for a routine check-up at City of Hope, Mom and I make the six-hour drive to Arizona for an interview. It's my first time back in the state since I got sick—another triumphant moment for me. And on a side victory, on the way to Flagstaff, we stop at Dad's house to stay the night. I want to go back to the house where my illness first revealed its ugly face. I want to confront it now, healthy as I am.

The next morning, Mom, Dad, and I gather at the kitchen table for breakfast. Geri is already a few hours into her shift at the hospital. Between bites of Eggos and sips of decaffeinated coffee Geri made before she left, it hits me: this is the first time I've had a meal with my parents since I was a baby. I savor the moment, thinking it will probably also be the last.

Dad has been extremely distant lately, and it's caused us to have a very superficial relationship. It always has, actually. I've tried talking to him about it, but he just blows me off, saying he's too old to have such an "emotional, drawn-out, frivolous" discussion with me. "I'm almost 70 years old," he keeps saying.

Dad, I just feel, has been fighting some demons his whole life, those more chilling than anything I've ever faced. One is regret over never pursuing his dream of designing cars after he won all those awards as a kid. Another is jealousy, most recently of Rod. I figured this out from a comment Dad made before I returned to Michigan.

Upset that I hadn't been in touch in a while, he said, "I'll bet you've been calling Rod."

And he was right, but it was because Rod actually *talked* to me. He didn't just ask me about the weather or the latest sports topic, then dish the phone off to Geri like it's a hot potato. (Geri, for her part, has never answered my pleas to talk to Dad for me, ask him to open up. I once asked Dad about his relationship with his father, thinking that would get him to open up. He told me it was "fine," offering no more. I told Geri about it, that I needed to know more, and she did nothing.)

Regardless of the situation with my dad, I still enjoy the breakfast I have with him and Mom. I suppose I've come to appreciate that at least my dad's still alive. Some people I know aren't that lucky.

Soon Mom and I make the two-hour drive north to Flagstaff for my interview. After checking in with the receptionist, I'm ushered to a conference room by the *Daily Sun*'s sports editor and assistant sports editor. (We are soon joined by the managing editor). There, we all discuss ideas for the sports section, the direction it can go. They listen to my suggestions, which are plentiful.

"Enterprising stories," I tell them, a buzzword I learned from my sports editor at the *Ann Arbor News*. This type of communication (and team atmosphere) is exactly want I want in a sports staff. I thrive in this environment, and it looks like they do as well. I am confident about my chances, and eagerly await the news back in Ypsilanti.

⊶ ▆◈▆ ⊷

About a week after my return home, I get the call.

"We all liked meeting you," Chris Lang, the *Daily Sun*'s sports editor, tells me. "You certainly have the qualifications. We've been talking it over and, if you want the job, we'd like to offer it to you."

I'm excited about the move; it's another fresh start. And the unknown has always greeted me well, like it did on my first trip to Michigan.

Surprisingly, Rod doesn't share my enthusiasm,

"Are you sure you're ready to go?" he asks.

What's he talking about? He initiated the move.

I would have never looked for another job, just a year after coming back, if he wasn't hightailing it to the Marines.

"Of course I'm ready," I tell Rod.

"I don't know. It's going to be tough."

Rod's right. This will be the first time I've lived alone since I moved into the dorms in the fall of 1998. But I have to go. I need to be on my own again, away from Rod, away from Jessica. I have always been anxious to see how I handle new situations, and this time is no different.

Reggie Jackson said he viewed every at-bat in his Hall of Fame baseball career as an opportunity to succeed, rather than a chance to fail.

This is my opportunity.

CHAPTER TWENTY-TWO

Field of Hopes & Dreams

—✦—

"The function of leadership is to produce more leaders,
not more followers."
—RALPH NADER

*I*n September 2003, Rod and I load up all of my things—along with the black leather furniture in our living room that Rod bought with his NFL signing bonus—into a U-Haul truck. Our destination: Flagstaff, Arizona.

After helping me move into my new apartment, about 80 miles south of the Grand Canyon, Rod accompanies me on my first day at work. Walking into the newsroom with him, it feels like show-and-tell day at school—I've brought a football player.

"Nice to meet you," Chris says, jumping out of his chair to shake Rod's hand. "Steve says you played with the Ravens. I watched the Ravens a lot out in Virginia, where I'm from. But the Redskins are really my team. I covered them as a freelancer when I was at Virginia Tech."

"Oh yeah?" Rod says, genuinely interested.

Show-and-tell ends quickly. Rod goes back to my apartment, and I get settled into my new work digs. I have a large, wall-less cubicle between Chris and Ed Odeven, the assistant sports editor and a proud Arizona State grad. It's a perfect location—right in the middle of the action.

The following morning, Rod and I greet Mom and Nana, who drove in to see my new home. The next morning, on their way back to Palm Springs, they drop Rod off at the airport. As they drive off, I realize I'm finally on my own again. Make the best of this opportunity, I tell myself.

Back in Michigan, Rod continues to train for the Marines. He keeps it up for weeks, but ultimately he's not able to realize his dream. His knees, upon further medical examination, are worse than he thought—practically bone-on-bone. He will not be part of that hierarchy he so misses, or follow in the footsteps of the military men in his family.

Rod tells me the news over the phone. "I wouldn't be able to handle the Marines physical right now any more than I would the Baltimore Ravens physical," he says.

As always, Rod just moves on from the disappointment: no fuss, no bitterness. I, on the other hand, was warming to the idea of my big brother, the soldier. I wanted to call him Major Payne, like the movie with Damon Wayans.

⊷ ⊷ ⋙✦⋘ ⊶ ⊶

After moving in with a friend in Ypsi for a few months—Rod and I had to give up our house after our one-year lease was up—Rod decides he's heading south, back to Miami. Shortly after Rod arrives home, he's offered a job to manage a popular fitness center in Fort Lauderdale, about 45 minutes north of Miami. He moves into a luxury apartment near the gym with his friend, Alex, a former Marine.

"It's a blessing," Rod tells me after he starts the job. "I'm going to make some major changes around here."

For the next few months, Rod trains clients and learns all the valuable business skills he needs to go along with his natural physical talents. He enjoys training clients so much, he says, that he has decided to do it full time.

Rod wakes up at five in the morning, meets with his clients by six, and gets more work done by 10 a.m. than I do all day.

I've seen Rod talk to young players before. It's one of the most amazing things I've ever seen: motivation at its purist level. Today, Rod doesn't mention coaching as part of his future plans, but I know it's somewhere in the works. It has to be.

"It's just good to be home," Rod says. "I need some time to reconnect."

<hr/>

Across the country, I continue to connect with my new surroundings. I continue to grow as a writer. I pen weekly columns on local and national sports, as well as report on northern Arizona's vast Native American culture and its many contributions to local sports. I also cover Northern Arizona University's varsity sports and chronicle the progress of its official Olympic training center. Flagstaff's 7,000-foot elevation rivals the thin air of Colorado Springs, which has traditionally led the way for Olympic training.

Best of all, I have the energy to do everything I want. This includes waking up at 4 a.m. the first Sunday in February 2004 and driving two hours to Phoenix Sky Harbor Airport. My destination: Houston, where I will cover Super Bowl XXXVIII at Reliant Stadium.

From the auxiliary media seating in the top deck, I watch another Michigan Man—Tom Brady—lead the New England Patriots to their second Super Bowl victory in three years, this time over the Carolina Panthers. A few years ago, I interviewed Brady during his first pro football game in the state of Michigan, when he was just fighting for a roster spot in New England.

Brady explained to me how difficult the transition from college to professional football was for him. Each night, he would take to the practice field after dinner with some of the other rookies, going over plays to be caught up for the next day's practice. After our interview, when his teammates loaded into the charter bus for the ride to the airport, I shook Brady's hand and asked him one more question.

"Wouldn't it be nice if we actually made something of ourselves someday, Tom?"

"It sure would," Brady said, nodding his head. "It sure would."

Two Super Bowl MVP trophies later, I think Brady has accomplished that goal. As for me, just working at the Super Bowl in Houston has brought me one step closer to achieving mine.

I hung out with Bill Plaschke in the press box before the game. And afterward, I interviewed Patriots receiver Troy Brown—right next to Michael Wilbon. (We took turns firing questions at Brown.) Those are the modern-day sportswriting legends that my old coworkers at the *Ann Arbor News* so respected.

But the highlight of my time in Arizona—by far—is that I'm finally able to answer Rod's question. "What's *your* story?"

My story runs on December 28, 2003, on the cover of the *Daily Sun*'s Sunday edition. It's about how I was able to overcome leukemia two years earlier with the help of my best friend, a former professional football player. For the next few weeks, readers stop me on the streets, at sporting events, even in restaurants, to comment on the story.

While eating a stack of pancakes at IHOP one Saturday morning, I watch a woman leave her table and walk toward me. She stops right in front of my table.

"Excuse me, but are you the reporter who wrote that story about the football player? The one who teamed up with you to fight cancer?"

"Yes," I say, standing up to shake her hand.

She informs me that her cousin has recently been diagnosed with leukemia.

"I found your story so inspirational," she says. "I'm thinking about showing it to her."

I offer her a seat, but she declines.

"No, thank you; my husband's right over there. I just wanted to say hello and tell you how much I enjoyed that wonderful story."

"Have your cousin call me if she ever needs anything," I say, handing her one of my *Daily Sun* business cards. "I'll be glad to talk to her if she wants. About anything at all."

I give out my phone number a lot in the next few months. By summer, in another unexpected twist, my story wins second place for feature writing by the Associated Press Managing Editors of Arizona (APME). A few weeks later, the lead photo of my story—a shot of Rod snapping the ball with a Michigan State lineman about to collide with him—is projected on a big screen at the 2004 APME banquet in Phoenix. I'm not in attendance—Chris makes me work that night—but some of my coworkers who were tell me it received a nice ovation.

During all of this, Rod is back home doing whatever he can to inspire people. A longtime member of the Fellowship of Christian Athletes, Rod speaks regularly at FCA events. The FCA, I learned after Rod sent me a program from a recent function he spoke at, brings together Christian athletes at all levels from all around the country to be leaders among their peers.

Eventually, I get to see one of Rod's speeches firsthand. In late December 2004, I fly to Miami to watch Rod speak at the annual FCA Orange Bowl prayer breakfast. In a hotel banquet room the size of a football field, we sit with coaches and players from the 2005 BCS national championship game, Oklahoma and USC. Rod's inspirational words make such an impression on Oklahoma head coach Bob Stoops, he asks Rod to host a private chapel service for his team, to take place at the Sooners' team hotel on the Sunday before the game.

"Guys, you're not just football players out there—you're leaders," Rod tells Oklahoma's players, as he paces the room with a Bible in his hands. "That comes with a great responsibility."

I sit to the side of the partitioned banquet room, a more intimate setting than the breakfast with the teams. At various points in the sermon, I look across the aisle at Jason White, the Heisman Trophy–winning quarterback from a year earlier. I watch him and his teammates focus intently on Rod, who's still pacing the room.

"Men, as leaders, you're going to be challenged. You're going to be tempted to go off-track," Rod says, then fingers through the book of

Genesis for a verse that supports his message. "It says in Genesis 3:1, 'Now the serpent was more cunning than any beast of the field God had made. And he said to the woman'—Eve—'Has God indeed said, 'You shall not eat of every tree in the garden?'"

"What did she say?" Rod asks the players. "'We *may* eat the fruit of the trees of the garden.' And that's where she succumbed: she was disobedient and then went and talked Adam into doing the same. What happened? God found out and punished them, a punishment we all still feel to this day."

Rod is referring to the pain of childbirth God levied on Eve, and the toll of mortality he gave to Adam.

"Guys, you can't take the bait—you can't be tempted by the fruits of fame and money or your obedience will be shattered. You'll be left naked—naked in faith—like Adam and Eve. This game will do the same thing to you—it will eat you up and leave you with nothing, if you're not careful. It says in Ephesians, chapter 4, 'We should no longer be children, tossed to and fro and carried about with every wind of doctrine, by the trickery of men, in the cunning craftiness of deceitful plotting.'

"Guys, you can't be led. *You* have to lead the way and show others how to do it as well. You have to play to inspire out there."

Those words, besides sending a chill down my spine like they did the first time I heard them, give me an idea. I flip over the pamphlet containing the weekend's itinerary and write:

Whatever you do . . . play to inspire.

You can be a preacher, like Rod is now—preach to inspire.

You can be a doctor, like Dr. Snyder—heal to inspire.

Heck, you can be a teacher—teach to inspire. A waiter—serve to inspire. Or a friend—be there to inspire.

After I return to Arizona, Rod tells me he's speaking to 1,500 kids a day during Black History Month. And a few months after that marathon of speeches, I call Rod to tell him my big news: I will finally be able to spread a message of inspiration and leadership that Rod has done so many times—on the field and off.

It's June 5, 2005: National Cancer Survivor's Day. Events are held all around the country. The administrators at City of Hope ask me to tell my story. The event, "Field of Hopes & Dreams," is held at City of Hope's campus in Duarte. I'll be one of two recent cancer survivors to speak to a crowd of nearly 2,000.

I prepare a 12-minute speech for the patients at various stages in their battle: either just starting it, nearing the thick of it—those really in the thick of it can't even leave their rooms—or celebrating their victory outright.

I went over the speech so many times outside of Mom's apartment in the days prior, pacing along Palms Boulevard as cars whizzed by, I memorized it word for word. It reminded me of when I played in the bands and sat in my bedroom for hours the day of a show, practicing my bass lines. When the lights went down in the club that night, and the band was introduced, I was ready to go.

My speech centers on using the people around you—your teammates—to help bolster you during the long fight—about how I had no choice but to do that because I knew I couldn't defeat my disease on my own.

"I learned a lot during this most recent cancer," I say, wearing a vintage California Angels jersey, my part in adhering to the baseball theme of the event. "Mostly I learned that I'm not alone in life. There are great people around me willing to help."

"Rod was my team captain," I inform the crowd, "but you need more than just one teammate to win a championship. I needed my doctor, my mom, other family members, friends, and all of the nurses and administrators at City of Hope, many of whom are here today."

This, I know, is my opportunity to thank these people, along with that angel halfway across the world—whom I now know personally. I met Annette a couple months ago, when City of Hope flew her in for its annual bone marrow transplant survivors reunion. Annette doesn't speak English, so we communicated through a translator. Despite the language barrier, we felt like a brother-and-sister team reuniting after a three-decade separation. City of Hope even flew out Annette's fiancé, Franz, who was just as wonderful as his future wife. It was their first trip to America.

As for my speech, I close it by saying, "Let's all team up and achieve victory." People stand up and give me an ovation. The crowd even applauded during key points in the speech. As the sound system booms Gloria Gaynor's "I Will Survive" to close the event, people start to approach me.

"You're such an inspiration," they say.

"You've helped me get ready to tackle my disease," they tell me.

One woman says, "Thanks so much for sharing your amazing story."

"It's not *my* story," I tell her. "Teamwork is about more than one person. Remember? I couldn't have survived without all the people I mentioned, including my fellow patients and their caregivers. People like you."

Shortly after the speech, Rod flies to Arizona. He and I load up another U-Haul with all of my things and drive across the country again. We move into a seaside condominium in Boca Raton, Florida. Rod found the place, just like he did our house in Ypsilanti.

"What do you think?" Rod says, as we exit Florida's turnpike into another world: sunny South Florida.

"Unreal," I say. "We get around, don't we?"

Rod's been urging me to move here since he returned home. Like before, I was very noncommittal. I felt like I just got to Arizona.

"We have to be together, man," Rod kept telling me. "At least we should live in the same city." I found it hard to leave my job and the foundation I built in Arizona. But after thinking about what's most important in my life, like I did in the hospital, it wasn't a difficult choice. I'll go where my brother is. Plus, my speech has showed me that I too have an ability to inspire people, and I don't need a press credential to validate me anymore.

Time to move on, find another surplus of new story ideas. And maybe more.

After allowing a couple weeks to get settled—and take my customary noontime spells on the couch—I start searching for another job. I find one as a universal desk editor at the Forum Publishing Group, which publishes some 28 weekly editions of the South Florida *Sun-Sentinel*.

Along with my work at the paper—some writing, some editing, some page designing—I give speeches at City of Hope events, mostly fund-raising dinners. There are plenty of them in South Florida: "chapters," as they're called, host them. Without these volunteer chapters, people like Dr. Snyder and Dr. Forman couldn't pull off the miracles they do. That is what I tell the people in attendance.

"Your efforts are not going in vain. I'm living proof of that. Without you, I wouldn't be here right now."

After the speeches, people come up to me and say some of the same things I heard after my speech in LA. (Others, I notice, break out pens and start filling out their checks to City of Hope. What a feeling to see that.)

As for Rod, this new season in his life is also reaping rewards. Upon taking a break from training clients to work in real estate a few months, Rod married the former Carie Diaz, a South Florida native he met at the gym. She came in for a job interview and got a whole lot more. I served as best man in their December 17, 2005, ceremony at the same Miami church Rod attended while growing up.

Following their honeymoon to Jamaica, Rod was offered a job as head football and wrestling coach at Westminster Academy, a regionally accredited Christian school a short drive down A1A. Rod's hire was reported a few days later in the *Sun-Sentinel*. The headline, simply read, PAYNE GOES TO WESTMINSTER. Rod left the mortgage business and returned to the gridiron, where he belongs.

One day after practice, Rod and I hung out on the porch of our first-floor unit of the condo, just a lime's toss from the water. I would soon move into an apartment nearby, to give him and Carie their space.

After talking for a while, I broke out the video of the speech I gave in LA.

Rod took a seat on the couch. He grabbed the remote and turned up the volume. I sat at the desk we bought at the furniture store in Ann Arbor. Rod was quiet during the speech, until one of its high points, when he suddenly leapt to his feet.

"Yeah, yeah!" he bellowed. "This is how we do things at Michigan!" Rod paused to hear what came next. He was still standing. "This is how we do things at Michigan," Rod repeated, this time softer as he sat back on the couch. "I'm proud of you, Steve."

Thinking about that, I got another chill—perhaps the biggest jolt I've ever felt after something Rod has said.

That's how we do things at Michigan.

This must be what a coach tells a player after he does something good on the field. I never would have heard such words of praise unless I was a player myself—a competitor like Rod, not some reporter sitting high up in the press box, judging those down on the field, and I'm reminded of Roosevelt's words: "It is not the critic who counts, not the man who points out how the strong man stumbled. The credit belongs to the man who is in the arena, whose face is marred by dust and sweat and blood . . . who in the end knows the triumph of high achievement; and who at the worst, if he fails, at least fails while daring greatly so that he shall never be with those cold and timid souls who know neither victory nor defeat."

While I have never been an athlete, have never worn the famous winged helmet and run out of Michigan Stadium's tunnel—I have walked down it, thanks to Rod—I do, at least, understand the meaning of those six words inside Schembechler Hall, the ones above the glass doors leading out to the perfectly manicured practice fields: THOSE WHO STAY WILL BE CHAMPIONS.

*"I am not a fan; a fan does not believe—he hopes.
I am a teammate, the one who has put in the time for
the team and knows what it means to give of himself
and his time and whatever else is of value to man,
that he may live and die, no matter what happens,
as part of the team. That I am: a teammate."*

—ROD PAYNE, JULY 2004

Acknowledgments

I would like to thank God, as well as Jesus Christ, my Lord and Savior, for giving me wings when I was falling. Forever thanks to Mom and Nana, my MVPs during my recent illness, as well as Myron Kamisher and Sandra Coller, the Kaplans, the Lavintmans, the Resnicks, the Nadels, the Feingolds, the Rosenzweigs, the Zatzs, the Copelands, and all of my family and friends who helped me achieve victory, including Dr. Anthony Zoppi and family, Mr. and Mrs. Austin "Rocky" Kalish, Jim Lantry, and Nellie Crawford.

Fond appreciation to Joyce Sweeney and her Thursday writing group, including Heidi W. Boehringer, a terrific writer and a fine photographer. Without their help, a good story might have never become "great." Endless praise to Jennifer Roberts, along with her little angels, Nick and Damian, for their unwavering support—and Jen's fabulous editing! And Ed Odeven, a former coworker and lifelong friend, for his editing and advising—you're a true pro, Ed.

Esteemed thanks to Dr. David Snyder and the miraculous staff at City of Hope, including Dr. Stephen Forman, who first answered my plea for help. Thanks also to Joan Wizner, Megan Hawn, and Paola Douaihi at COH Florida; Dr. Frances Valdes at Mercy Hospital, who is always on call when I need her; Dr. Luis Quintero and family; and Ms. Susan Nelson, the angel who flew to Germany to pick up my donor's blood.

To Annette Karrer, my bone marrow transplant donor. Without her, the biggest angel of them all, Team Rom's hard work might have been for naught. And to her children and wonderful husband, Franz:

we love you all. To our agents at Venture Literary, Greg Dinkin and Frank R. Scatoni, who recognized the potential of this story when others didn't. Special thanks to our editor, Mark Newton, along with the staff at Sports Publishing LLC, including acquisitions editor Noah Amstadter, who got the ball rolling on this project, and Dave Hulsey and Andi Hake, who kept the momentum going. Thanks to Pastor Bob Coy at Calvary Chapel Fort Lauderdale and Pastor Jim Burnett at Northland Christian Assembly Flagstaff for their inspiring messages and eternal hope, as well as Randy Wilson at the *Arizona Daily Sun* for allowing me to write the newspaper story this book is based on.

To Dad, who insisted I become a student at the University of Michigan ("in Ann Arbor") even when the verdict was still out on Notre Dame—and for taking me to all those sporting events when I was a kid; and to Geri, for all those egg-salad sandwiches on the flights to and fro. To Linda and Carie Payne and the rest of the Diaz and Payne families; Jessica and Gae Jacobs and all of the Jacobs family, especially Norman and Ruth; Matthew and Laura Hausle for their love and constant guidance; Bryan and Liz Beam for their special friendship and amazing Web work; Nick Iarussi for a lifetime of laughs; David Ablauf and the University of Michigan athletic department; Per H. Kjeldsen and Ronald J. Heys for assisting with photos; Patrick M. Gleason and the Baltimore Ravens; Larry Stewart, Bill Plaschke, and Bill Dwyre of the much-respected *LA Times* team; and Rick Frishman, Sharon Farnell, Deborah Kohan, and the amazing team at Planned Television Arts for taking this book to the next level.

A heartfelt thanks to Geoff Larcom of the *Ann Arbor News*, who believed from the beginning that I could do "anything," as well as the rest who inspired me along the way: John Lowe; Arthur Gallagher; Ron Matthews; Fritz Breidenbach; Brian Curtis; Dr. David Ganz; Dr. Anthony Daly and Los Angeles Sports Medicine; Sid and Beverly Kline; Professor Julie Davey; Jeanne Lawrence; Mercey Lemos; Jean Blaylock; Linda Baginski; Angie J. White; Annie Watson; Kevin Koga; Norman Goldstein and Mary Irwin; Elizabeth Terry; the nurses at the "university research hospital"; Sid and Bobbie Johnson; Kevin McQuinn and family; Yodit Mesfin; Christine Pechera; Julie

McKenna (Go Green!); Erin O'Dwyer; Jesse Anderson; Jorge Flores Rodriguez and Alex Ferrari of the film *Broken*; Marly Goldberg; Miriam Silverberg; the Kanters; the Crows; the Nieters; the Mirandas; the Wickas; the Rennings; the Councils; the Durcos; the Dunitz family; Frank Phillip and family; Ashley Reichenbach; Demetrius Smith and family; Mike Brennan; Tim Martin; Dave McVety; Mr. and Mrs. Steve Warns; the Heuers; the Strohmans; Brian Caldera (and Bobby); Brian Maizuss and family; Red and Lois Simmons; Robert MacGregor; the Rosens; the Plockis; Sue Guevara; Coach Hutchins and the (2005 National Champion) Michigan softball program; "Hi" Hideki; Angela Vargas and family; Julie Buehler; Jim Rutherford; Glenn Johnson; Mrs. Shannon Pennington; Jim Coleman; Matt Meyer; Dan Williamson (great skater photos); Stephen J. Dubner; David Ratner; Rusty Shelton; Jason Keith and the Alpha Kappa chapter of Pi Kappa Phi, notably Jeffrey S. Brink, Ryan Proud, and Tim Gerber; Pam Doto, Nick Powell, and all at Forum Publishing Group; Armando Vega and the PsychicMafia crew; Coach Sam Scarber and family; Barry Acquistapace; Andrew Oshiro and family; Wali Waiters; Ed Shaland and family; David Den Herder and the rest of the *Michigan Daily* sportswriters; Tony and Carrie Forsyth; Leisa Thompson; Lon Horwedel and family; Brian Reynolds; Arny Mackowiak; Janet Storm (thanks for the framed picture); Karen Tonogbanua; Jack Gillard; Joanne Hoeft; David Goricki; Marc Sasso and family; Dr. Imran Iqbal; Bill Stimming and family; Fay Zak; Josie O'Donnell; Bunny Osborn; Katherine Pryor; Kimberly Herezi; and Becky Rogers—along with Crystal and Alex (Play "2" Inspire).

Lastly, thanks to Rod Payne, who saw something in me I always wanted to see in myself—a competitor. Without him, I would merely be a critic right now, and I can't think of a sadder ending to my story.

—STEVE ROM

Acknowledgments

+—◄◊►—+

First, I would like to thank my Lord and Savior Jesus Christ for choosing a sorry, knuckle-headed misfit like me to give his unimaginable grace, mercy, and love. Nothing I have accomplished can be attributed to how good of a person I am. The love I have for my family, friends, and teammates comes from one place—Jesus Christ. Thank you for being my true source.

Thanks also to my mother, Linda, for all she has done for her only child. In this country, raising a young black male to love and not hate is an accomplishment that no words can describe. Thank you for not hating my father for his absence from our life: that's the only reason I can love my dad with a clear heart today. Whether he says it or not, I know he feels the same way. Your love and your commitment to raise me in the eyes of God is the sole reason for my success. Your biggest reward is yet to come.

To my family, thank you. Grandpa, I'm sorry you never got to see me play in college or win the Super Bowl, but that's OK. Grandma took notes and will fill you in on the details when she gets to heaven. Grandma, you are the "virtuous wife" from Proverbs 31:10. Uncle Neuman and Aunt Velma, thank you for some of the greatest memories a young boy can have. Nothing beats hot rods and motorcycles. Uncle Warren and Aunt Diane, thank you for "keeping it real." Besides, every family has a little insanity. Uncle Sherman, I love you, no matter what! To all my cousins, it's our turn now. Let's make sure we give our children what we were given: hope, love, and sacrifice.

To Coach Miller, thank you for showing me that the words *coach* and *father* are one and the same. Because of you, I stand a little more tall and firm. Your lessons of school pride and loyalty stay with me always. You too, Mrs. Miller; your kitchen and heart were never closed. Thank you.

Thanks to the state of Michigan! They say every man has a place where his heart runs wild and adventure waits. For me, it's Michigan. Florida is my home, but Michigan is my heart. The University, fall colors, deer season, pheasant hunts, and cool summer lakes—I long for your embrace. Despite your cold snowy winters, this country boy can survive. Brent, Lori, Matt, Tyler—I love you guys.

To the University of Michigan, thank you. Bo, Gary, Lloyd, thank you. To Cam Cameron and family, thank you for recruiting me. We've come a long way from neighborhood gunfire and recruiting trips. Les Miles and family, as an offensive lineman, I owe almost all of my skills and technique to you. I believe you're one of the best—thank you. To my trainer, Todd Yager: I love you, man. If Humpty Dumpty had you when he fell, he would've been back on the wall in no time. You are in our prayers. Bruce Dishnow, where do I begin? Your walk with Christ was my safety rope in a sometimes-hopeless college atmosphere. You were truly needed. Thank you so much. To the rest of my coaches and teammates, thank you. Jarret; Fish; Ed; Che; Harold; Elston; Amani; Mercury; Windt; Damon; Biakabatuka; Griese; Riemersma; Marinaro; Jansen; Adami; Denson; Buster; Ben Huff (RIP); Chuck; Ty Law; Woody Hankins (I'm sorry); Trezelle . . . all my brothers!

Mike Gittleson: the greatest strength coach to ever live. Andre the Giant has a posse.

Thanks to the Cincinnati Bengals, Paul Alexander, and Bruce Coslet, for showing me how bad a program and its coaches can be.

A special thanks to the Baltimore Ravens, Art Modell, and Coach Billick, for renewing my faith that a program gives a player every chance to succeed. Perhaps that's why we're World Champs, hm?

To my wife, Carie, I love you and pray we have a fruitful life and marriage. Thank you for putting up with me. Thank you for your support. We've just begun. To my little girl, Isabella, Daddy loves you! To my unborn child, I'll see you soon.

Last, but certainly not least, I'd like to thank my brother from another mother. Steve, I said, "I got your back," and I meant it. Despite your quirks, you are the best friend a guy could have. That's why I couldn't let you die in that hospital. I love you, bro.

—Rod Payne